SAVE MORE THAN YOU EXPECT

5 APPROACHES THAT CAN HELP YOU SAVE $10K+ ANNUALLY

BENJAMIN TAYLOR

A SPECIAL GIFT FOR MY READERS

Included with your purchase of this book is our Bonus Content,

7 Ways to Challenge Your Self-Control.

This booklet is a training for you to try with small day-to-day habits before you move on to making big changes in your life.

These mini challenges can help you improve your health, live minimalistically and can help you save more money!

Click the link below and let us know which email address to deliver to

https://benjamintaylor.activehosted.com/f/1

CONTENTS

Introduction	ix
1. THE COMMON OBSTACLES OF LIFE	1
A Rising Debt Problem	3
Dwindling Financial Literacy	5
Increasing Financial Stress	8
The Importance of Financial Self-Awareness	11
Final Word	14
2. THE KEY TO OVERCOMING FINANCIAL OBSTACLES	15
How Habits Work	16
The Basics to Developing Habits	20
Some Possible Bad Habits to Look Out For	26
A Personal Story	31
Final Word	32
3. THE FIRST APPROACH: KEEP THE DAY JOB… FOR NOW	34
Why You Should Keep Your Day Job	35
Final Word	38
4. THE SECOND APPROACH: THE SPENDING DIET	40
Why You Need to Know What You're Spending Your Money On	41
The Most Common Unnecessary Expenses of the Modern Person	45
Methods That Can Be Implemented to Cut Back on Unnecessary Spending	51
A Personal Story	55
5. THE THIRD APPROACH: SAVING CHALLENGES	57
365 Days Saving Method	59
52 Weeks Saving Method	60

26 Weeks Saving Method	61
How Much Money Should You Really Save?	62
A Personal Story	63

6. THE FOURTH APPROACH: MONEY HERE, MONEY THERE — 65

Personal Cash Flow Analysis	66
The Basic Rules of Budgeting	73
Dealing with Debt	77
A Personal Story	82

7. THE FIFTH APPROACH: CUT DOWN ON AVOIDABLE EXPENSES — 85

Why You Need to Cut Back on Your Expenses	86
Before Spending, Ask Yourself These Five Things	90
Fixed Expense vs Variable Expenses	94
Personal Story	98

Afterword	99
A Special Gift For My Readers	103
About the Author	105
References	109

© **Copyright 2021 - All rights reserved.**

The content contained within this book may not be reproduced, duplicated or transmitted without direct written permission from the author or the publisher.

Under no circumstances will any blame or legal responsibility be held against the publisher, or author, for any damages, reparation, or monetary loss due to the information contained within this book, either directly or indirectly.

Legal Notice:

This book is copyright protected. It is only for personal use. You cannot amend, distribute, sell, use, quote or paraphrase any part, or the content within this book, without the consent of the author or publisher.

Disclaimer Notice:

Please note the information contained within this document is for educational and entertainment purposes only. All effort has been executed to present accurate, up to date, reliable, complete information. No warranties of any kind are declared or implied. Readers acknowledge that the author is not engaged in the rendering of legal, financial, medical or professional advice. The content within this book has been derived from various sources. Please consult a licensed professional before attempting any techniques outlined in this book.

By reading this document, the reader agrees that under no circumstances is the author responsible for any losses, direct or indirect, that are incurred as a result of the use of the information contained within this document, including, but not limited to, errors, omissions, or inaccuracies.

INTRODUCTION

You may have already heard of the old adage that your habits build your character. Everything that you are and have in life now is only the result of the collective habits that you have practiced all throughout the years. And the person that you want to become in the future can only be built through a specific set of habits that you practice faithfully today. Whether you choose to believe it or not, this is a principle that applies to every facet of your life. If you want to be fit and healthy, then you need to consistently practice habits that promote nutrition and wellness. You need to eat the proper food in the appropriate amounts. You also have to maintain a regular fitness and exercise regimen. If you want to be more proficient at a specific skill, like playing the guitar, for example, then you need to enforce good habits in the way that you devote time and energy to your practice. You must always employ good habits if you want to be a good student, a successful employee, a responsible parent, or whatever endeavor you might come to think of. But for this book, in particular, we are going to delve into the habits that you need to achieve true financial independence.

Money is a complicated matter because not many people are open to having conversations about their finances. It's such a sensitive and taboo topic that isn't always so freely discussed out in the open. This is the reason that a lot of people who experience financial woes just keep their problems to themselves. There's a certain stigma that's attached to people whose financial situations are in disarray, as if it's something to be completely ashamed of. So, instead of talking to other people in an effort to find solutions to their problems, these individuals will try to sort things out themselves, even when they barely have the faintest idea of what to do. That shouldn't really be the case. Money problems are very common among many people. And these problems can't be solved merely by sweeping the issues under the rug in the hopes that things eventually just fix themselves. That's certainly not how it works. It's important that people develop better relationships with their approaches to handling finances. People need to maintain healthier mindsets when it comes to talking about money in general and that's something that this book is going to address.

Think of this book as a conversation about your finances. It's not going to merely be an instructional guide to help you balance out your bank statement. It's a book that strives to help you develop a more constructive mindset when it comes to dealing with your money. Whether you realize it or not, the kind of mindset that you have when it comes to finances is crucial to you achieving your financial goals. Many people make the mistake of thinking that money is merely a matter of pluses and minuses. Yes, it's true that money is essentially just mathematics on the surface, but it's also much deeper than that. More than anything, money is about psychology. You need to develop the kind of mental fortitude that is necessary for you to make smart and sound financial decisions. You could be incredibly skilled at arithmetic, but that will do very little if you still consistently make poor financial choices.

Earlier, we talked about how your habits eventually end up building your character. But there's a precursor to that. It's your mindset that ends up determining what your habits are going to be. Without the proper mindset and the knowledge that you need to make informed decisions, then it will be impossible for you to consistently enforce good habits. So, this book is going to break everything down to the root of your financial woes. Regardless of whether you're someone who is deep in debt and looking to claw your way out, living paycheck to paycheck and barely able to make ends meet, or if you're someone who is just generally anxious about what your future financial situation is going to look like, there will be something for you in this book.

It can be very jarring having to deal with your financial woes while knowing that you don't have anywhere to turn. That's why this book can serve as both a source of comfort and knowledge for you. Whenever you start to feel overwhelmed by all of your problems, know that you're not alone. There are many others who are in the exact same boat as you. In fact, there are even many who have had it worse than you and managed to find success for themselves in the long run. You just feel helpless now because it seems like you don't currently have the tools that you need to better your situation.

It's true that dealing with financial problems can be very intimidating. It's not an easy feat. Achieving financial independence is something that has managed to elude so many people in the past. But the good news here is that it's not an impossibility. It doesn't matter what kind of financial situation that you're currently in. As long as you're equipped with the right mindset, you will always have the potential to develop a proper game plan that will help you achieve eventual financial independence.

1

THE COMMON OBSTACLES OF LIFE

"I'm broke."

"Bills. Bills. Bills."

"I can't afford it."

"I can't find a job."

"How am I going to retire?"

*S*ound familiar? You might have found yourself saying these things before. At the very least, you've encountered people who have been saying these things over and over again in life. This is the common language of people who are in financially compromising situations. You would never find a financially independent person proclaiming that they're broke or that they don't have money to pay the bills. A financially independent person wouldn't be worrying about having to find a job or figuring out what they're going to do about retirement. If you've found yourself saying phrases like these before, then there's a good chance that you've been in a financially strained position. And it's very important that you admit this to yourself at the start.

The first step to solving a problem is recognizing that there is one. You can't overcome credit card debt if you just continually ignore it. You won't be able to curb your shopping addiction if you just keep on pretending that it doesn't exist. You will never be able to rid yourself of bad financial habits unless you first recognize that they're there. That's why it's essential for you to get real and honest with yourself. Admit that you have a problem and that there's a need for you to change it. If you're perfectly fine and content with your life, then that's okay. That's your prerogative. But if you've been uncomfortable with the way that things have been playing out and you are desperate for something new, then you might need to change a few things.

This chapter aims to open your eyes to the many problems you might be facing right now. A lot of people seem to lack the self-awareness that's necessary to pinpoint the challenges and obstacles that they're facing in life. That lack of self-awareness is what often resigns people to merely sticking with their current lifestyles even when they're not happy with it. The sad fact of the matter is that many people subject themselves to leading mediocre lifestyles that fail to give justice to their potential. Think about how many people are told that they just need to go to school, graduate, find a job, work until retirement, and then wait until their lives come to a conclusion. Of course, that isn't to say that there aren't people who fail to derive a sense of meaning and fulfillment with this kind of life. But for a vast majority of people, this is merely a formula that they're given very early on and are forced to stick with. The problem with this kind of framework is that it doesn't allow much upward mobility and room for growth. Instead of people learning how to better empower themselves financially, they're just taught to be good employees and hope for a chance to eventually earn a wage that's big enough to support their lifestyles. That's the number one mindset that you need to address today. You are never going to achieve the life that you want on a single stream of income alone. But we'll talk more about that later. For now, you just have to recognize that there's a problem with the way that people typically look at life. Specifically, we will be delving into some of the most common obstacles that people face when trying to achieve financial independence.

A RISING DEBT PROBLEM

There's an alarming debt crisis that is currently sweeping the United States at the moment. While the country is busy grappling other important issues like the global pandemic, economic recession, and inequality, it almost seems like no one is talking about the debt problem anymore. As of January 2021, the total consumer debt in the United States is estimated to be at around $4.2 trillion (Amadeo & Estevez, 2021). That is by no means an insignificant amount. However, the good news is that the debt hasn't ballooned much over the course of the pandemic-stricken year. But there's also a bad side to this. It also means that more and more people are afraid to borrow money to fund businesses and other investments that could potentially stimulate the economy. For the purposes of this book, we are only going to address the kind of debt that most people have trouble dealing with:

- Credit Card Debt
- Student Loans
- Auto Loans

Credit Card Debt

The first major kind of debt that most people currently face is credit card debt. Researchers have found the median debt for American families currently amounts to roughly around $2,700 while the average debt hovers around $6,270. Overall, credit card debt in America is estimated to be as high as $807 billion among 506 million credit card users. To rich people, having around $6,000 in debt might not sound like much of a big deal. But for the lay worker who lives paycheck to paycheck every month, this kind of debt can seem almost insurmountable. Again, this is just the debt that you can get from credit card purchases. Typically, the most common items that people purchase with credit cards include fashion items, vacations, groceries, and basic utilities among other things. The more troubling statistic that we haven't touched on here is the fact that around 45.4% of American families have some kind of credit card debt. That's almost half of the population who find themselves unable to settle their credit card bills at the end of a billing cycle. (Resendiz, 2021)

Student Loans

Forbes magazine came out with an article in February 2021 stating that the total student loan debt in the United States has risen to a whopping $1.7 trillion. To put things into perspective, student loans account for more than 40% of the total consumer debt of the country. The concept of student loans has always been a tricky one. Again, we touched upon this earlier. In life, most people are conditioned to think that they need to complete formal schooling in order to secure a good job that will set them up for life. And this is true for a lot of people. However, another big truth is that most people don't have the means to afford college. This is why a lot of students end up taking on debt way before even getting any assurances at a stable wage. A lot of students graduate college without a job and are already burdened with hundreds of thousands of student loans. Since these loans are so big, the interest rates make it more and more difficult for students to pay them off. Very few companies would pay top-dollar for fresh graduates, and students don't have the money to pay off their student loans right out of the gate.

Auto Loans

The current statistics for auto loans in the United States are reaching record numbers. This might not typically be what you would have expected considering the effects of the pandemic in 2020. But to paint a clearer picture, Americans currently owe around $1.4 trillion in total auto loan debt. You might not think that to be a big number considering the costs of automobiles these days, but try to wrap your head around this. More than 2.3 million new auto loans are taken out each month. This means that 2.3 million cars are being sold to indebted consumers on a monthly basis. That amounts to $56 billion of debt every single month. And these auto loans don't even take into consideration the additional expenses that come with owning a car such as parking fees, gasoline, and maintenance costs (Jones, 2021).

DWINDLING FINANCIAL LITERACY

Aside from dealing with increasing debts and expenses, a lot of Americans are just plainly financially illiterate. It's obvious that the level of a person's financial literacy directly correlates to the state of their finances. It's already a given that people will face various financial obstacles in life, regardless of who they are or what backgrounds they have. It's just that people who are financially literate are in much better positions to weather these storms and overcome these challenges effectively. Conversely, people who are financially illiterate are more likely to make poor financial decisions that could ultimately destabilize their financial situations. And make no mistake about it, there is a significant financial literacy problem in the United States today.

Currently, only 4 out of 7 Americans are deemed to be financially literate while just 24% of millennials have a good understanding of basic financial concepts (Fu, 2021). These are crucial statistics because it reveals a lot about why so many Americans are struggling with their finances. Being financially educated will equip one with the tools, knowledge, and confidence for proper money management and strategy.

Unfortunately, there are just way too many people who have either very misinformed or underdeveloped understandings of finance. Not all people understand what an emergency fund is or what the differences between fixed and variable expenses are. These are basic financial principles that everybody should learn and understand. And yet, that isn't the case. These are all telltale signs of a lack of financial literacy among the general public.

What Is Financial Literacy?

To put it simply, financial literacy is the amount of knowledge that an individual has on financial, credit, and debit management. This knowledge is necessary for anyone to make sound and rational financial decisions, particularly when it comes to saving, spending, budgeting, and investing.

Financial literacy can be manifested in the way a person decides to set up a monthly budget or how someone decides to grow and invest their hard-earned money. Financial literacy is a crucial skill that many people need to learn as they work their way towards achieving true financial independence. Financially literate people tend to also be those who are more likely to be able to buy houses, pay for childrens' college, and retire early.

Regardless if you live in rural or highly urbanized areas, not developing your financial literacy can dramatically impact your mobility in life. Yes, it's true that money can't buy you happiness. But having money can definitely afford you the mobility that you need to generate more opportunities for happiness. Don't make the mistake of thinking that only low-income earners are guilty of being financially illiterate. There are many high-income earners who fall into financial woe precisely because they are financially illiterate. Conversely, there are low-income earners who lead relatively comfortable lives because they are good at handling their money and they always make the right financial decisions. The level of someone's income is not always indicative of a person's financial literacy.

Why Is Financial Literacy Important?

First off, it's becoming more and more apparent that consumers need to ensure their own financial security without having to depend on charity or welfare. In previous generations, everyday workers relied on pensions and social security in order for them to gain some kind of financial security for life after retirement. However, it's becoming increasingly evident that the amount of money that social security can provide is no longer sufficient for modern lifestyles. When it comes to planning for the future, it's imperative for younger workers to be thinking ahead and making financial decisions that will allow them to be comfortable in retirement.

Next, trends show that a huge chunk of the population seems to be unprepared when it comes to dealing with unexpected occurrences and emergencies. This was especially made evident when the COVID-19 pandemic came rolling around. It was estimated that more than half of millennials lacked a proper emergency fund to help get them through rainy days. Establishing an emergency fund is one of the most basic principles of financial literacy and yet, many still haven't equipped their war chests with the adequate amount of cash.

Lastly, the financial landscape is continually changing and evolving to become more and more complex every day. With the emergence of block chains and cryptocurrency, the world of investing is changing rapidly. Any failure to keep up with emerging financial trends would render people at a disadvantage when it comes to using their money wisely in this modern age. Even something as simple as participating in the stock market is quickly becoming democratized among the mass population. It's now a lot easier than ever for people to start investing in stocks. But since many don't have a firm grasp over the concept of investing due to a lack of proper financial literacy, they don't capitalize on this opportunity to have their money work for them.

INCREASING FINANCIAL STRESS

Financial stress is no joke. Depending on your financial situation, the amount of finance-related stress you experience could have as significant an impact on your life as you may have initially thought. Think back to a time wherein you checked your pockets or your bag to suddenly not find your wallet where it's supposed to be. It's almost like experiencing a mini-heart attack, isn't it? But that's just a small matter, especially if you realize that you've just placed your wallet somewhere else. Even in those instances, the stress can already be dramatic. Now, imagine the kind of stress that can come from much bigger things like not knowing how to pay for rent at the end of the month or not knowing where your next meal is going to come from.

It's a sad reality for many Americans that they struggle with finance-related stress on a daily basis. And even though most peoples' days might only be composed of small doses of stress, they can eventually add up and start to compound into a much more serious problem. According to a study that was spearheaded by Dr. J. Galen Buckwalter, there is a certain mental disorder that is currently afflicting the lives of 23% of Americans called Acute Financial Stress or AFS (Brooks, 2016). This is a disorder that is defined to cause dramatic negative impacts on a person's thoughts, feelings, and actions. Experts say that it has effects that mimic those of Post-Traumatic Stress Disorder or PTSD. And the worst part about being afflicted with AFS is that it could completely destabilize a person and render them incapable of fixing their stressors and financial woes to begin with.

Some of the symptoms of being afflicted with AFS include:

- Insomnia
- Feelings of isolation
- Anxiety
- Hypervigilance
- Emotional numbing
- Reliving of past stressful events
- Avoidance, etc.

Stress Made Worse by the Coronavirus

It's undeniable that one of the biggest stressors and financial obstacles that people have had to face all over the world is the COVID-19 pandemic. In an article published by CNBC, it was reported that almost 90% of Americans felt anxious about their money, according to a survey conducted by the National Endowment for Financial Education (Fox, 2020). In another survey conducted by The Harris Poll, it was found that 41% of Americans were worried about not having an adequate retirement fund while another 23% were worried about their retirement (2020).

Throughout the pandemic, there were many things that placed stress on Americans including rent, mortgage, and utility bills. But this is the most interesting statistic: it was found that stress levels among the general public were the same across all income levels. Everyone was dealing with financial stress as a result of the global pandemic. What does that tell us? That means that it doesn't matter how well-off or comfortable you already are. You are still prone to experiencing financial stress every once in a while. What's important here is how you handle that stress to maintain your composure and ensure that your finances stay intact while in the midst of an emergency.

Fortunately, it's been reported that more Americans have decided to be more intentional in the way that they handle their money. According to the same CNBC article, around 75% of Americans have taken the necessary steps to remedy their financial situations since the start of the pandemic. Around 42% of people have said that they made deliberate efforts to cut down on their expenses while 26% of people have delayed making drastic financial decisions like big purchases and investments. Ultimately, stress can strike anyone at any given moment. It doesn't matter who you are. It's just important that you equip yourself with the tools that you need beforehand to deal with these stresses appropriately.

THE IMPORTANCE OF FINANCIAL SELF-AWARENESS

To conclude this chapter, it's prudent to go back to the main point of you taking the time to really know what you're up against. Again, there's no way for you to solve the problem unless you know what you're facing. This is why it's important for you to develop some sense of financial self-awareness. You need to be aware about what your current financial situation is so that you can devise a game plan moving forward. Unfortunately, this book can't tell you what your problems are. This is something that you need to do on your own through reflection and introspection.

The simplest definition of financial self-awareness is essentially a person's knowledge of their own financial assets, liabilities, and spending habits. You need to develop your self-awareness with your finances if you want to gain better control over your expenditures and your investments. A lot of people who just mindlessly handle their finances think that they're doing things right. They have good intentions when it comes to their money. They know that they shouldn't be spending more than their means and that they should be investing a bulk of their money. However, good intentions alone are not enough. Think about it. No one ever intends to go into credit card debt. No one ever intentionally seeks out money problems. These are things that happen gradually and quietly. These bad money habits build up over time and compound the problem until it becomes too big to ignore. If you have a developed sense of financial awareness, it becomes a lot easier to sniff these problems out just as they're developing. This way, you can cut them off right as they're forming and remedy them easily.

It all goes back to the simple truth about how financial responsibility is really a psychological endeavor. You might think that you want a life of comfort and luxury. But if you don't have the kind of mindset and plan that will help you get from where you are to where you want to be, then it's all moot. You won't have the motivation and the blueprint to actually pursue your financial goals and aspirations. Developing your financial self-awareness will lead to you becoming more intentional in your approach to handling your money. Self-awareness leads to structure and purpose with the way that you do things.

Simple Steps to Developing Your Financial Self-Awareness

The more you read through this book, the more you will develop your self-awareness as you go. But here are a few general tips that you need to keep in mind. These are just four gentle reminders that you have to live by and you will be on your way to developing your financial self-awareness.

Practice Proper Planning

The old adage, "Failing to plan is planning to fail," always applies, especially when it comes to finance. You need to develop a proper plan in terms of handling your finances if you really want to become financially independent. Developing a plan forces you to become aware of different variables surrounding your finances like your income, expenses, debts, and investments. When you have a plan, you add more structure to the way that you handle your money. Every move that you make becomes purposeful and is in service to a particular financial goal that you have.

Obsess Over the Littlest Details

You need to be as detail-oriented as possible when it comes to overseeing your finances. You might think that paying $5 for parking or $2 for a tip at the bar doesn't really matter. But it's the little expenditures like this that can really add up over time. When you learn to be obsessive about even these littlest details, it becomes a lot easier for you to identify both where your money is coming from and where it's going. The most financially independent individuals in the world always have a great eye for detail when it comes to their financial habits.

Spend With Your Mind and Not Your Heart

You must already be familiar with the concept of impulse buys. Let's say that you've had a rough day at work and you've decided to have dinner out with some friends on the weekend to let off some steam. You see a really expensive bottle of wine on the menu and you think that it's worth splurging on because you deserve it for all of the hard work that you've been putting in. That is called an emotional purchase. You are spending money based on how you feel. Often, it's these kinds of purchases that can really lead to poor financial decisions. Another example is when you're heartbroken over a setback at work or in your home life. So, you decide to take a stroll through the mall and you find a nice pair of shoes. You think that buying the shoes will buy you happiness and a temporary escape from your problems. Again, this is another emotional purchase and it's not always a wise one. It rarely ever is.

Emphasize Saving Over Spending

Lastly, you need to emphasize the idea of saving over spending. Too often, people will just relegate saving to something that happens once all the expenses are accounted for. It's often placed at the back of one's mind. In other terms, people tend to take a more passive approach to the idea of saving. This is a big mistake. You always need to be more active in your savings. One easy way to do this is to set aside a huge chunk of your monthly salary and dedicate it to savings. Then, whatever is left behind will be used for your expenses. The way that most people do it is wrong. They take their income and use it to pay their expenses first, and then they decide to save if there's anything left over.

FINAL WORD

Developing your financial awareness is only one very small but important part of becoming financially independent. Again, the whole point of this chapter was to orient you on the many obstacles that might be keeping you from achieving your financial goals. This is why financial awareness is so crucial. We've just barely scratched the surface when it comes to you really pushing for your goals. But this is a good start. This chapter should have opened your eyes to the harsh realities that are in front of you. This way, you have a good grasp of what you're up against and what you need to do moving forward.

2

THE KEY TO OVERCOMING FINANCIAL OBSTACLES

In the previous chapter, we talked about the things that may be keeping you from actualizing your financial goals. We also briefly touched on the idea on how building a proper mindset and practicing good habits are crucial aspects to your financial development and management. In this chapter, we are going to take a deeper dive into the idea of how impactful your habits truly are. You will learn more about how habits can truly change your life for the better or worse, depending on your approach to building them.

Aside from that, we will also be talking in-depth about how you can build better habits for yourself. Unfortunately, habits are not mere items that you can purchase at a store. Building habits in life require a certain level of discipline and commitment. You need to make sure that you dedicate proper time and energy into the formation of these habits in order for them to truly stick. Again, this is not going to be an easy process, but it isn't entirely impossible either. With the help of the insights from this chapter, you will be on your way to building some really good habits that will help create a positive impact on your life.

Lastly, this chapter will also point out some of the probable bad habits that you might be doing. We already talked about how good intentions alone are not always good enough. You need to reinforce your good intentions with good habits. More importantly, you need to be policing yourself from practicing bad habits. With the help of this chapter, you will get more information on what kinds of bad habits most people are guilty of committing, so you will be in a much better position of not doing the same thing.

HOW HABITS WORK

It's important to preface the rest of this segment by saying that there is no magical formula that will instantly allow you to become better at life and develop good habits. Building habits aren't easy, but they're most definitely worth it. We'll get to developing your habits later on. For now, it's important for you to understand why building good habits is important to begin with and how it's going to shape your life for the better. Sure, there are a lot of people who adopt the kind of lifestyle that enables them to make decisions on a whim and to live life a little recklessly. The truth is that that kind of lifestyle really does work for some people. However, for most individuals, it pays to establish a healthy routine that's composed of good habits to build a quality life.

Have you ever looked at people who are *hyper*productive in life and wondered how they manage to get so many things done? Think about people like Barack Obama, who was so busy running a country and also happened to have been writing a book on the side. How did he have the time to do that? Think of guys like Elon Musk and Mark Cuban, who dip their hands in different businesses and companies every day. How do they find the time to manage all of these different aspects of their life and still find success? The truth is that it's all in the routine. Human beings are psychologically wired to crave comfort. There is a lot of comfort to be had in the routine and the predictable. It can be so unnerving, stressful, and anxiety-inducing to have to wake up everyday knowing that you have to build everything from scratch. However, when you have a routine, it creates a sense of order amidst all the madness. It doesn't matter how many things you're doing in life. If you establish a routine that works for you and you manage to stick to it, you will end up being productive.

If you fail to set up a proper routine, it can be so easy to get distracted by things that are of little to no importance. Having a set routine essentially wires your brain to act mechanically. You become more efficient at identifying the tasks that need to be accomplished. You also gain better proficiency at accomplishing those tasks over time. By establishing solid routines that are built on good habits, you will be able to shape your life and your environment in a way that promotes your own efficiency and productivity. This is a principle that doesn't just apply to finance. It's applicable everywhere.

Routines in Decision-Making

The best part about practicing good habits to build a solid routine is that it helps you focus on the things that will actually help you get to where you need to be. All of the unnecessary things and distractions become a lot easier to block out and ignore. Ultimately, your habits will form a system that is designed for you to succeed in the long run.

Just think about the number of decisions that you're forced to make on a daily basis as a functional human being. The moment you wake up, you are forced to make a decision as to whether you should get up or go back to sleep. Then, you need to decide if you'll take a bath or have breakfast first. If you'll have breakfast, you have to choose what you cook. All of these micro-decisions can pile up and exhaust your mind and brain power throughout the day. However, by establishing a plan, a set of habits, and a proper routine, you take away the problem of having to make these decisions on the spot.

Take, for example, your first decision of the day—whether to wake up or go back to sleep. If you have a routine that forces you to wake up at 4:30 a.m. every day to exercise, then that's a decision that's being made for you. If you wake up at 4:30 a.m., you just automatically get up without thinking if you should go back to sleep again. This is because it's already been laid out in your routine and you just naturally flow into it.

Developing Habits to Serve a Purpose

It's very important to emphasize that developing habits and routines should always be in service to a particular goal or purpose. For example, if you're making a habit of waking up at 4:30 a.m. every day and you just end up spending most of your time mindlessly browsing through social media, then the routine in itself doesn't add much value to your life. However, if you decide to wake up at 4:30 a.m. every day so that you have extra time to exercise in the morning, then that is an example of a routine serving a purpose. It's the same with your finances as well.

It's not enough that you merely make it a habit of saving your money. You need to be saving your money for a purpose. It's not enough that you develop a routine of checking your monthly expenses, you need to do so for a purpose. All of the good financial habits that you build should always be geared toward a financial goal because this is crucial to helping you stay motivated. Again, it's not easy to practice good habits. It's a lot easier to fall into bad habits and that's why a lot of people go through financial woes. But if you understand the *whys* of your habits and your routines, then it becomes easier for you to stay on track with what you're doing.

Differentiating Important Tasks and Urgent Tasks

How many times have you experienced ending a day feeling so tired and drained while also feeling like you didn't really get that much done? It happens way too often to a lot of people and not many can pinpoint why. Well, ultimately, it's because a lot of people fall into the trap of expending a lot of energy on urgent tasks as opposed to important tasks. There's a significant distinction between the two. Important tasks are essentially the specific micro-goals that you need to accomplish every day in order for you to meet your greater goal in life. Urgent tasks are these random little errands or nuisances that require your attention throughout the day which you might not have been able to prepare for.

For example, if you work as a journalist, your important tasks for a typical work day might be to do research for a particular story, interview a witness to a crime, or write out an article that your editor has assigned to you. These are all important tasks that are in service of you wanting to become a better journalist. However, throughout the day, some urgent tasks might also require your attention. For example, during the day, you realized that your hair is getting long and so you schedule a haircut for yourself. In the afternoon, you remembered that you needed to pick up your drycleaning from the laundromat. So, you keep in mind to leave work early so that you can get to the laundromat before it closes. It's the little tasks like these that can make up most of your day and take valuable time away from your important task. They still require a certain amount of energy, but they don't necessarily serve your larger goal. That's why you end up feeling tired at the end of the day even though you also feel like you didn't accomplish much.

But where do routines fit into the picture? Establishing a routine will help you stick to the plan of only focusing on the important tasks at hand. The only tasks you would incorporate into a routine will always be the most important ones. If you follow your routine efficiently, then it becomes a lot easier to feel fulfilled and productive at the end of the day. Of course, you should still carve out some time to perform the urgent tasks, but most of your time should be spent on your priorities in life. Your routine just helps pinpoint which things to prioritize and which things you can work on later.

THE BASICS TO DEVELOPING HABITS

Building habits is not an instantaneous process. It's not something that you can accomplish after just one try. It's a continuous process that you need to work at and sharpen as you go. But sometimes, not everyone knows how to go about starting a proper habit. So, if you feel like you don't know how to develop good habits and stick to them over time, don't worry. You're not alone on that boat. There are so many people who try to start developing good habits only to abandon them in the long run because they approach it in the wrong manner. Here are a few basic foundational steps that you can take as you try to build good habits for your own life.

Start Off Small

A lot of people try to go big or go home, and they end up going home as a result. Of course, it's important for you to be ambitious, but that doesn't mean that you need to make drastic changes in your life right away. When developing new habits, it's okay for you to take baby steps. Make some very small changes in your life that will allow you to gradually ease into the routine that you really want. You need to allow your body some time to get used to the new way you want to do things going forward. This goes for anything. If you want to lift weights, you don't start lifting 300 lbs. You would start off as a beginner and use the 10 lb dumbbells before benchpressing that heavy. This will take time to build your muscles and gradually your body will adjust to the increase in weight as you workout more.

Maintain a Positive Disposition

Don't start out expecting that you're going to fail. Always maintain a positive disposition. Make sure that you believe in yourself and in your capacity to get things done. It can be so hard to accomplish a goal if you're incapable of visualizing a version of yourself that's succeeding at it. Visualize your success. Really believe in your ability to get things done. This is a crucial step to starting things off on the right track.

. . .

Commit to Your Convictions

Always make sure that you actually commit to your convictions. Once you decide to make a change to your life, then stick to it. There's no room for backtracking here. It can be very tempting to second-guess yourself during the initial parts of the process, especially when the results aren't always apparent right away. This is why you need to just trust in your convictions. Really stick to these habits knowing that they're eventually going to pay off in the future. The first parts of developing a new habit is crucial because it's what ignites the momentum that's necessary for you to sustain this habit in a daily routine.

Identify Your Obstacles

Another important step you need to take is to identify your obstacles. We already talked about this in the previous chapter. But just to emphasize it, whenever you set a goal for yourself, you can't pursue it blindly. You can't just assume that everything is going to be so easy and smooth for you. It's imperative that you take the time to sit down and reflect on what your greatest challenges are going to be. You must look to your goal and determine what impediments are keeping you from success. Once you identify these hurdles, it becomes easier for you to not just anticipate but also to prepare for them whenever they do come.

Develop a Plan for Success

Next, you need to develop a plan for yourself. Again, we already talked about this earlier. But planning is crucial because it gives you the roadmap toward success. Again, it's not enough that you have certain ambiguous goals. It's not enough that you have the desire to be better. It's not enough that you are motivated to succeed. You also need to know what steps you need to take to get to where you want to be. This is where the planning process comes in. When developing your habits, try forming a daily plan that you can stick to, which will help you stay consistent with your habits. Try to eliminate the margins for error as much as possible.

Make Room for Failure

Next, you have to try to make room for failure. The road to success is not a smooth one. You are going to encounter a few bumps in the road. For example, if you're trying to make it a habit to eat more healthily, it's not always going to be possible. There will be times wherein certain circumstances will make it too hard for you to resist slipping. During these moments, it's important to not beat yourself up too much over it. You're still human and you're still prone to these kinds of setbacks. Instead, just acknowledge that you've made a mistake and try to learn from it moving forward. Don't let one mistake serve as a cause for you to abandon the plan altogether.

Get Support From Your Loved Ones

"No man is an island," as the old adage goes. Keep in mind that even though your financial journey is a very personal one doesn't mean that you have to go through it alone. You can always recruit the help and support of the people around you to help keep you honest. This is especially true for your loved ones who are deeply invested in your overall well-being. Open up to them about the change you're trying to make in life and let them know how they can help you out. Getting that kind of support when you're faced with adversity is crucial to you sticking to the plan and staying consistent.

Celebrate Milestones, Both Big and Small

Celebrate your wins, no matter how big or small they might be. Always acknowledge any tangible signs of progress that you make. Even something as simple as going two straight months of paying your credit card bill in full is an achievement to be proud of. Or perhaps going a full week without spending on any unnecessary expenses. These are all signs of progress and they must always be given recognition. Remind yourself of the results of your hard work so that you are further incentivized to keep on staying disciplined with your practicing of good habits. You have to take it upon yourself to be your own biggest cheerleader. You should always be proud of your own personal achievements.

Put Yourself in an Environment for Success

A lot of the time, people are mostly molded by the environments that they are in. People who put themselves in environments that are toxic and that don't enable growth tend to fail. On the flip side, people who surround themselves with an environment that is nurturing and opportune also tend to be the ones who succeed. In life, you need to surround yourself with the right people if you want to develop good habits. By doing so, you would be placing yourself at the best possible position for success.

. . .

Remind Yourself of Why You're Doing This

Undoubtedly, just because you've built good habits over time doesn't mean that things are going to get easier as they go. You just get better at dealing with adversity because of the proficiency that you've developed with your routine. However, there are still times wherein you will find yourself tempted to revert back to your old ways. During these moments, you must always remind yourself of your motivations. Remind yourself of your progress so far and how good it feels to actually find success in your goals. But most importantly, remind yourself of the reason that you've decided to change your life in the first place. Find that motivation within you to continue to stay the course and stay disciplined.

Be Patient

Of course, you must be patient. "Good things take time." Even aged wine or aged cheese are more decadent than the newly processed ones. The best things in life don't come easily and they always take time. This is especially true when it comes to finance. Nobody overcomes a huge amount of debt in a day. Nobody gets rich over just the span of a week. When you're changing your life for the better, it can be so easy to seek instant gratification, but it isn't always going to be there for you. Sometimes, it's going to take a long while before you can really see the fruits of your labor. That's why it's crucial for you to stay patient at the start. Just because you don't really feel the progress taking place within you doesn't mean that it isn't happening. You're still moving forward and that's the most important thing. The results will come over time so long as you stay consistent.

. . .

Take It One Step at a Time

Lastly, just take it one step at a time. Don't shoot big right away. Don't be too greedy. Always recognize your limits. If you're incapable of making drastic changes all at once, then don't force yourself. Everyone moves at a different pace. You need to go at the pace that best suits you. Make sure that you develop your own rhythm as you continually pursue success. Just take it one step at a time as you slowly start to adopt a new lifestyle for yourself. Then, you can start picking up the pace as you go along. But when you're just in the first phases of this lifestyle change, don't be so eager to leapfrog the process.

SOME POSSIBLE BAD HABITS TO LOOK OUT FOR

It's not easy to break habits once they're already so ingrained into your system. That's why it's best to sniff them out when they're just starting to form or just avoid starting them altogether. But again, that's a lot easier said than done. Sniffing out bad habits can require a great deal of self-awareness that not many people have. More importantly, not many people always recognize what a bad habit is supposed to look like. To conclude this chapter, we're going to talk frankly about some of the bad habits that most people tend to make when it comes to managing their own money. Some of these habits may already apply to you and some may not. That's okay. If they apply to you, then you need to make a conscious effort to make some changes to the way that you do things to ensure that you break these habits as fast as possible. If you aren't guilty of these bad habits, then that's good. Continue to police yourself in this regard. Stay disciplined and make sure that you never allow these habits to form and be given life in the first place.

You Spend More Than You Earn

It's just a matter of simple mathematics. Spending more money than you earn is not going to help you save money in the long run. This kind of mindset will always lead to you having a negative balance on your income statement. This is why budgeting and expense tracking is so important. You need to know just how much money you're spending and earning at the same time. This way, you always know how to control your money movement in a way that benefits you. If you're spending more than you are earning, then you need to do either one or both of these two things: cut back on your expenses or increase your income. You can cut back on your expenses by making a list of things that you spend money on which aren't really all that necessary. You can also increase your income by looking for side hustles or asking for a raise or promotion at work. Either way, you have to find a way to ensure that you never spend more than you earn at the end of the month.

You Take Out Payday Loans

Payday loans are one of the worst forms of debt that you could possibly ever take on. A lot of people will resort to payday loans whenever they're tight on money because they need immediate access to cash in order to pay bills or any other kind of emergency expense. However, what you need to realize is that there are other forms of loans that you can take which are more financially sound than payday loans. Usually, payday loans are very convenient and banks make it easy for their clients to take these loans out with minimal hassle. Although, these loans also carry outrageously high interest rates. In the long run, you'll end up putting yourself in a worse financial position than when you started. As much as possible, avoid taking out payday loans and seek alternative forms of instant access to cash.

You Don't Build an Emergency Fund

When you first start earning your own money, the very first thing that you need to do is build your emergency fund. That's the absolute priority. If you don't have an emergency fund yet, then that should be the first item on your list when you get your paycheck at the end of every month. The ideal emergency fund differs from person to person. However, a good goal to shoot for would be to have at least three to six months' worth of expenses in cold hard cash that's readily available for you to access. You can place your emergency fund in a savings account with a bank and never touch it unless a rainy day comes along. Too many people find themselves in precarious financial situations because they don't have emergency funds to fall back on whenever something unexpected happens. For example, you could get laid off from work or someone close to you might have a sudden illness. You'll need money on-hand to help weather that storm whenever it strikes. If you don't have a prepared emergency fund, you might end up having to take a loan and you'll plunge yourself into debt.

You Only Pay the Minimum on Your Credit Card Bill

Credit cards in themselves aren't inherently bad. That's something that you have to realize as early as now. There are many dramatizations of credit card debt on popular media wherein people start cutting their cards up and throwing them into the garbage. Of course, if you don't have the kind of self-control and discipline that's necessary to properly use a credit card, then you might as well not have one. But having a credit card can actually be very beneficial, especially if you make use of 0% installment promos and rewards bonuses. Credit cards only become a real problem when you keep on swiping them even though you don't have the money to pay them off in full at the end of every month. People seem to think that merely paying the minimum balance on a credit card is okay. On the contrary, that's poor use of credit cards because they tend to carry some ridiculous penalty fees and interest rates. You'll end up paying a lot more money than is necessary if you just keep on paying the minimum every month. Make sure that you only use your credit card if you know that you have the capacity to pay your debt in full at the end of each billing cycle.

You Blame Other People for Your Financial Woes

Unfortunately, there are too many people out there who refuse to take responsibility for their financial situations. They are so quick to pass the blame to other people when it comes to their financial woes. Of course, their grievances might be valid. No one ever intends to put themselves in a precarious financial situation. You would never wish upon yourself a life of debt. But there's a serious problem when you continuously blame other people for your troubles, because it does nothing to appease the situation at all. You are merely trying to rid yourself of guilt, but the problem is still going to be there. And it's still going to be up to you to solve it. So, regardless of whose fault it is, you really need to own up to your financial problems. You must confront them and face them head on if you are ever going to get over them. That is the only way that you're ever going to overcome them in the future. There's no way that you will be able to achieve true financial independence if you keep placing the accountability and responsibility on the shoulders of others.

You Leave Your Savings in the Bank

It's good if you leave your emergency fund in a savings account within a reputable bank. Again, it's important that your emergency fund is readily available and accessible. That's the kind of convenience that a savings bank can provide you. However, the problem with placing *all* of your money in a savings account with a traditional commercial bank is that you end up losing money in the long run because of inflation. The interest rate at which your money in a commercial bank grows is never going to be high enough to outpace inflation. So, the hundred dollars that you have in the bank now isn't going to be of the same value in five or ten years. It won't have the same kind of spending power. That's why you should look to alternative vehicles of investments for your extra money. Look to bonds, trusts, or stocks so that your money has a chance to grow and possibly even outpace inflation in a passive capacity.

You Hoard Money Without a Purpose

Ultimately, you should still see money as a tool. Money in itself is not the goal. It should always serve a specific purpose. You can be financially responsible and use your money to build an emergency fund or a retirement fund. You can invest your money in insurance or in the stock market. You can also use your money to set up a business that will help make you even more money. But also, it's okay for you to use money to have fun and splurge a little bit. Part of being financially responsible means knowing when you have enough money that will allow you to live a certain lifestyle. Take a vacation. Buy that nice watch. Invest in a nice piece of jewelry. Again, the goal of making money isn't just to have a lot of money. All of that cash in itself is inherently valueless unless you know where to invest it.

A PERSONAL STORY

A few years back, a friend of mine called me to rant about how much he hated working at his nine-to-five job. He said that he was growing frustrated with the kind of lifestyle that he had and he felt like he was stagnating. Somehow, he could sense that he wasn't maximizing his potential and that his company was keeping him back from being the person he wanted to be. He got the idea to start a business of his own and he wanted me to partner up with him. At first, I was intrigued so I asked him what his plan was. He said that he planned to quit his job so that he could focus all of his time and energy into the new business. This shocked me at first, but that's not all that he said. He also mentioned that he wanted me to do the same. My friend asked me to quit my job and make some very drastic changes in my life, including uprooting myself, just to build this new business from the ground-up.

After he said that, I immediately knew what my answer was going to be. I politely declined him because I knew it didn't make any good sense for me to risk it all on a business that hadn't existed yet. At that time, I knew more than enough about business to know that the failure rates of start-ups are very high and that it would be foolish for me to pour all of my eggs into a single basket like that. Also, I knew that it would have been much more feasible for us to maintain our jobs and work on the business as a side hustle. If he had been open to that idea, then maybe I could have considered partnering up with him. He was just demanding too much from me even when the prospects of the business succeeding were very slim. That was one of the hardest conversations I've ever had with a person. My friend was very persistent and he spent three full hours trying to convince me to partner up with him. But my resolve was strong. I asked if he was open to the idea of me partnering up on a part-time basis and he wasn't willing to budge either. Again, I politely declined and wished him well. He wasn't happy with my decision and he hung up on me. He even told me that I would regret it.

Fast forward to a year later and his business ended up hemorrhaging so much cash that he was forced to close it down to cut his losses. He also ended up having to go back to his nine-to-five to pay off some of his debts for his business. The two of us never talked about that business ever again.

FINAL WORD

By now, you should probably already be convinced of the powers of habits. You should know that the way that you structure your routine can have a significant impact on the way that your life is going to turn out. Keep in mind that success is not something that comes on a whim. It doesn't arrive out of the blue. All of the greatest achievements in life always come out of intentional efforts that are organized in such a way that promote efficiency and productivity. This is why it's absolutely vital for you to establish habits that make up a healthy routine, which will always allow you to perform at your best. Otherwise, it's going to be a lot more difficult for you to find success in whatever endeavor you might have.

For the next phases of the book, we will be talking about the specific and concrete approaches you can take to improve your current financial situation. These approaches are ultimately going to help you practice better habits and build a more wholesome routine for yourself. Whenever you feel like the information is getting a little too overwhelming, don't fret. Remember that it's okay for you to take things a step at a time. Change doesn't always have to be so radical and revolutionary. You can ease into things so that you can make sure that you're doing it properly. It's impossible for you to rush success and there would be no point in you trying to do so.

With that, make sure that you also constantly remind yourself of why you're sticking to these habits. Stay true to your convictions and internalize your motivations. This is what is going to help you stay consistent on your path as you fight your way toward achieving true financial independence.

3

THE FIRST APPROACH: KEEP THE DAY JOB... FOR NOW

If you have a day job and are thinking of making a change in your life, don't make any drastic decisions right away. Just because you eventually want to work your way toward financial independence even when you're not working from nine to five doesn't mean that you have to tender your resignation immediately. Having a day job is a blessing in this day and age. There are many people out there who are struggling to get any kind of stable income. This is why it's crucial for you to not abandon your source of income so quickly. If you're going to be truly financially independent and secure, then you need to build a financial war chest. The best way to build a financial war chest is to save as much money from as many income streams as you can produce—your day job being one of them.

In this chapter, we are going to talk about everything that you need to do in order for you to lay the groundwork for financial independence while still staying at your day job. Of course, over time, it will get to the point wherein you will be able to venture out on your own and possibly be your own boss. You could start your own business and dictate all of your working hours. But in order for you to have the freedom and flexibility to do that, there are certain financial goals that you need to meet first. This chapter is going to help highlight some of those goals so that you are better prepared to go after the life that you dream of.

You might be eager to get started on your dream life and career, but again, you need to be patient. You can't achieve everything right away. There's a very thorough and meticulous process that you need to undergo in order for you to do things right. Yes, you can slowly wean yourself out of your corporate nine to five, but make sure that you understand what you're getting into first.

WHY YOU SHOULD KEEP YOUR DAY JOB

Yes, you should always work toward being independent and self-sufficient when it comes to your finances. You don't want to spend the rest of your life just slaving away, working for the same company just for you to be able to sustain yourself. You eventually want to get to a point in life wherein you can dial things back a little and have a little more control over your time. That's fine. No one can blame you for having such aspirations. But it wouldn't be wise for you to just abandon your day job without having a proper exit strategy. Your financial independence hinges on the state of your livelihood. And if you don't have money coming in or you don't have sufficient savings, then you will effectively be putting yourself into a bind. That's only going to further complicate things. If you need to further understand why maintaining your full-time job is important, here are a few reasons:

You Need to Build Your Savings

It's going to be a lot easier to build your emergency fund by sticking to your corporate job than by going out and venturing into a business on your own. This is especially true for people who are novice entrepreneurs. The harsh truth is that people rarely ever succeed at business right away. If you aren't in a financial position to endure some losses at first, then you're going to find yourself struggling to stay afloat. This is why you need to build a solid emergency fund and perhaps even a sizable capital war chest that you can infuse into your business. Be patient and build your funds first. Your patience will eventually pay off in the long run.

You Need a Viable Business Plan

Next, you need to develop a viable business plan before you venture into anything concrete. If possible, try to find an accomplished mentor who can help guide you through the process. Maybe you can partner up with someone who has a lot of experience in business. You can't just leave your day job even though you don't have a plan for what you're going to do. Again, you need a solid exit strategy in place. Keep in mind that the moment you leave your job, your income is going to stop. This means that you'll be bleeding money. If you don't have a solid business that can help sustain you, then you're going to be eating up your emergency funds fairly quickly and significantly.

. . .

You Still Need the Insurance of a Corporate Job

Unfortunately, if you're your own boss, then there are certain perks that a stable employment at a proper company will not be able to provide you. For instance, when you're working at a proper company, you're likely to be getting a lot of great benefits like medical, dental, vision, and life insurance. These are things that you won't necessarily have when you're just starting up a business of your own. Some companies even offer comprehensive retirement plans for their employees. Sure, you get to enjoy the perks of being the boss, but you also lose out on all the perks of being an employee too. Don't just think about everything that there is to gain from being on your own. Think about everything that you would have to give up too.

You Need to Lay the Groundwork for Your Business

Another reason that you should stick to your corporate job for the meantime is that you haven't laid the groundwork for your business yet. Ideally, by the time you quit your day job, you already have a business that has been solidly operating for at least a few months. Again, a lot of people who start a business for the first time are prone to running into a few roadblocks and challenges. You are bound to encounter a few setbacks here and there. That's why it would be best for you to iron out the kinks of your potential business while maintaining your employment. Once you're confident that you have a solid business up and running, then you can actually start considering leaving your job. There's no harm in trying to play it safe.

. . .

You Need to Diversify Your Income

Lastly, maintaining your day job will allow you to diversify your income. There are many entrepreneurs out there who run successful businesses of their own and still have day jobs. This is because a common best practice in finance is always to have a diverse and varied income stream. As they say, you must never put all of your eggs in one basket. That way, if one basket falls, you still have a bunch of other eggs that you can rely on. It's the same with your income. In case one income stream runs dry, you should have at least one other stream that will help keep you afloat and sustain you.

FINAL WORD

It's okay if you're dreaming about eventually becoming your own boss. That's a very nice and noble dream to have. No one is going to fault you for that. However, you still have to be pragmatic in your approach to achieving such a goal. There are many people all over the world who share this dream, and yet, they find themselves stuck in a corporate job or doing some kind of work that they're not entirely happy with. However, they stick to their current paths because they know that it's the safe and responsible thing to do. That's why a lot of people really stick it out doing jobs that don't give them any sense of fulfillment or meaning. That's not something to look down upon. There's nothing wrong with wanting to be pragmatic. But there is a way for you to be pragmatic while also pursuing your dreams. You just have to get creative with the path that you take toward achieving it.

Yes, there are a lot of different challenges that you need to prepare for and overcome as you try to work your way toward financial independence. For instance, time is a major factor. How do you expect to build a full business on the side if you're still working from nine to five? That's something that you're going to have to work at as you go along. With proper discipline and time management, you would be surprised at how much you can get done within a day. You just have to stay focused and committed to your goal.

THE SECOND APPROACH: THE SPENDING DIET

This particular chapter is going to delve into more personal matters that a lot of people might be sensitive about. The reason why a lot of people are apprehensive when it comes to talking about their finances is because they feel a certain sense of innate guilt or shame about their spending habits. There are a myriad of reasons why a lot of people spend more money than they need to. For some, it's to fill an insatiable need to have all the nicest and newest things. For others, it's merely to impress the people around them. There are also those who turn to spending as a kind of therapy. The problem with this kind of approach to spending is that they are all emotional in nature. They are all rooted in a person's feelings and they aren't always the smartest financial decisions. That's why, in this chapter, we're going to get hot and heavy with the truth about spending and what specific changes you need to make to the way that you use your money.

To put it simply, this chapter is going to help put you on a kind of financial diet. Think about dieting when it comes to food. The reason that you diet is because you want to make sure that you stay healthy and maybe even lose a few pounds of unnecessary fat in the process. You cut down on the calories and you only eat what is essential. All of this is necessary for you to develop a caloric deficit so that you end up losing weight. You only eat as much as you need to sustain your body and it ends up becoming a lot healthier. However, if you don't go on a diet, then the converse effects can take place. You can be poisoning your body with a lot of unnecessary calories and unwanted fat. This will lead to weight gain and other corresponding complications like heart disease and diabetes. That's why it's essential that you consistently reassess what you're eating and how much of it you're taking in. This is so you can ensure the overall health and wellness of your body.

It's all the same with finances as well. If you're only spending as much money as you need, you will find that it's going to do wonders for your financial situation. You would be surprised at how much money you're mindlessly spending on things that aren't really necessary or don't add much value to your life. The best way you can avoid unnecessary spending is when you decide to get intentional about it. You have to choose to only spend on things that are absolutely necessary. Your wallet has to be led by your mind and not your heart. If you're feeling confused about how you should go about it, don't worry. This chapter is going to walk you through that entire process step-by-step.

WHY YOU NEED TO KNOW WHAT YOU'RE SPENDING YOUR MONEY ON

Many money experts will tell you that the quickest way to become bankrupt is to not pay attention to what you're spending your money on. No one in their right financial mind would be able to refute that saying. If you find yourself continuously in debt, then there's a serious problem with the way that you handle your money. Even if you're not in debt and you still find it difficult to have any real savings despite the fact that you have a steady income, it tells a lot about your relationship with your finances. As much as possible, you want to be more mindful of what you're spending so that you can prevent any impending financial downfalls.

The worst part about not being intentional with your spending is not realizing how much money you're wasting on useless things. Even during the course of a month, you can be constantly throwing money at little things that aren't really useful. During those moments, you might think that they're not causing much financial damage. But over the course of a month, those little things add up and eat away at your budget. For example, think about how much money you're periodically spending on throwaway items like gum, cigarettes, sodas, and other small things that you might find at your random convenience store. You might not think much of these things when you're buying them, but at the end of the month, you realize that you don't have any savings because most of your money went to the *little things*.

Establish Better Financial Control

One reason you need to know what you're spending your money on is that it gives you better financial control. If you stay on top of what you're spending, then that means you aren't merely giving into your emotional impulses. You are staying mindful and in control of where your money goes. This can go a long way in rehabilitating your bank account and ensuring that you always stay aware of everything that's going on with your money. Remember that the main reason why a lot of people get into bad financial situations is because they don't even realize that what they're doing is wrong.

Hold Yourself Financially Accountable

Another reason why you need to be more mindful about your expenses is that it allows you to be more financially accountable. Earlier, we talked about how people who have losing mindsets when it comes to finance are those who don't hold themselves accountable to their own money problems. They try to find scapegoats and other people to blame their own woes on. However, if you are doing a better job of really focusing on your spending, then you eliminate that possibility of having to blame others. You get to hold yourself accountable because you are the only one in full control of the movement of your money.

Track Your Progress

Once you start adopting a more intentional mindset when it comes to spending your money, you will gradually start to see your financial situation improve. You will see that your unnecessary spending will go down and your savings will go up. Or, you might see that even though you've tweaked your spending habits, you're still not hitting your financial goals. Either way, you're developing better awareness over the state of your finances. You can see if you're making substantial progress and if your methods are actually working. But you can also see if there's still more room for improvement in the way that you're handling your money.

Keep Your Money Organized

Organization is key when it comes to making sure that your finances are always on point. This is especially true when you start diversifying both your income and your investments. If you have more than one source of income, you need to know how much money you're getting from each specific source. When you're also investing your money in different investment vehicles, you need to know how each of these investments are doing and how much you've already put into them. You would never be able to keep track of these things if you weren't organized with your finances. And the only way you can be organized with your finances is if you pay more attention to your money's movement.

Ease Your Financial Problems and Stress

We've already talked about how a multitude of people are plagued by finance-related stress. It's not good for you to be bogged down by your stressful situations. Exposing yourself to so much stress can be extremely detrimental to your overall health and wellness. However, if you pay closer attention to your spending habits, you will find yourself doing better in your financial practice. This, in turn, will lead to an improved state of your finances and will ease the stress in your life. More than that, seeing the progress you make can be very therapeutic and motivating.

Reduce Unnecessary Spending

Naturally, a byproduct of paying closer attention to the way you spend your money is you reducing your unnecessary expenses. When you take your spending seriously, you will be forced to seriously reassess what your priorities are in life. It's so easy to just bypass the dollar amounts of the things that you buy. But when you take the time to sit down and think about the true value of these expenses, then you get a better idea of what your financial priorities are. For instance, do you really need a subscription to YouTube premium? Do you really need to spend $50 on coffee every week? These are just a couple of questions that you can ask yourself to determine if your money is going to valuable causes.

Avoid Getting Into Debt

Lastly, and maybe, most importantly, really zeroing in on your spending can keep you from going into debt. If you're already in debt, then the very first thing you need to do is make sure that you don't get deeper into debt. Either way, you can really stand to benefit from being mindful of the way that you spend your money. Again, no one ever intends to fall into debt. A lot of the time, it's mindless spending that gets people into these troubling financial situations. But you can easily avoid that just by making sure that every dollar you spend is only spent on the essentials.

THE MOST COMMON UNNECESSARY EXPENSES OF THE MODERN PERSON

It costs money to be alive. That's just a plain fact of the world. You need money to pay for rent or property to live on. You need money to pay for food and water. You need money to buy clothes, pay for transportation, and get an education. Everything costs money. Everywhere you turn, you're shelling out a certain expense, and that's fine. It's part of the social contract that we signed into by choosing to be a productive member of society. We pay for the goods and services of other people while also offering our own personal services and skills for a set income. Expenses in themselves aren't necessarily bad. That's the first thing you need to understand. The only bad thing about spending is when you're using your money for unnecessary things, and that's what we're going to talk about in this segment.

The fact of the matter is that people are prone to spending money on things that don't really matter or are just plain unnecessary. That's fine if you're rich enough and have the luxury to shell out large sums of cash on these things. But if you're barely able to keep a budget together, it's not wise to be splurging on these unnecessary expenses. The point of this chapter is not to make you feel bad about spending your hard-earned money on certain luxuries. You're deserving of treating yourself every once in a while *if* you can afford to do so. But if you're still in the process of balancing your account and building your wealth, it might be best to stay disciplined and stay away from these unnecessary expenses for now. Here are a few of the most common unnecessary expenses that most people are guilty of having:

- Subscription Services
- Pets
- Luxury Fashion Items
- Alcohol
- Takeout Food
- Uber/Lyft/Ride-Halling Services
- Vacations
- Entertainment

Subscription Services

The first thing that you need to take a look at are your subscription expenses. Sure, if you look at your subscription services one by one, it can be very easy to convince yourself that the prices are fairly reasonable and that you can afford it. You tell yourself that it's okay to spend $50 on a PlayStation plus account. It's not too much. Then, you add another $10 for a Spotify Premium subscription. Add $10 more for a basic Netflix account. You might be an avid bookworm and so you pay another $10 for an Audible account. After that, you realize that your Netflix doesn't have enough options, so you spend another $15 on an HBO Max account. Individually, it might not seem like you're spending all that much. But then, if you look at it collectively, you're spending almost $100 a month on these subscriptions. Again, if you can really afford to spend that much on luxuries like these, then that's okay. But if you're strapped for cash, then you may want to consider cutting down on these subscriptions for a while.

Pets

This might hit a little close to home, especially if you're an animal lover. But there's just no escaping the fact that having a pet can be really expensive. There are just too many things to account for. Of course, you have to account for the routine expenses like pet food, shampoo, vitamins, and the other usual stuff. You might also have to spend for occasional visits to the vet which can get really pricey. If you have a high-maintenance pet, then you'll need to fork up a lot of cash for grooming services. While having a pet can be an incredibly enriching and fulfilling experience, it can often drain your finances.

Luxury Fashion Items

This is another kind of expense that can be a really sensitive topic for a lot of people. There are many people out there who think that buying the cheapest clothes on the market is the best way to save money. But that isn't necessarily true. A lot of the time, these cheap clothing items can break down fairly easily and you'll end up having to replace them often. It might come out that you spend more money replacing these cheaply made clothes than if you just splurged on a nice luxury item. That's why the most financially sensible thing to do would be to spend a little more money on a quality piece of clothing. Don't calculate the price of the item as it is. Instead, calculate for the cost per wear. If you buy a $20 pair of jeans that you'll have to replace year after year instead of splurging on a $100 pair of jeans that will last you at least a decade (assuming that you'll maintain your weight), then it's a no-brainer. Go for the item that offers you better cost per wear.

But there's another layer to this too. It can sometimes get to a point of diminishing returns with the clothes you buy. There are so many designer brands that charge exorbitant amounts of money for mediocre pieces just because of their branding and marketing. This is no longer a wise investment and it doesn't make sense to spend your money on this.

Alcohol

Alcohol is a luxury. It should never be seen as a necessity. Alcohol can get really expensive because of a couple of things. For one, the sin taxes that are applied to commodities like alcohol or cigarettes make them more expensive than they have to be. Another reason that alcohol can get very expensive is their addictive properties. You don't really need alcohol to survive, so it shouldn't count as a necessity. Again, this isn't to say that you're not allowed to indulge in alcohol. It's just that if you're trying to stay tight with your budget, then alcohol shouldn't really be on your regular list of monthly expenses.

Takeout Food

It doesn't matter how tasty or how cheap takeout food might be. It's always going to come out cheaper if you just cook your own food. Keep in mind that part of what you're paying for when you buy takeout is the convenience of not having to prepare that food on your own. This is why companies will really hike up their margins when it comes to the food that they serve. They have to pay their workers and maintenance fees in order to keep their businesses running. The food itself doesn't cost as much as they charge. It might be a hassle to have to prepare your own food all the time. But it's certainly going to be a lot easier on your bank account.

Uber / Lyft / Ride-Hailing Services

Depending on where you live, transportation can get really expensive. And even though it can be really tempting to just take Ubers or Lyfts to work every day, you would be surprised at how much of your budget this habit is actually eating up. Haven't you ever wondered why these companies make it so easy and convenient for you to book a car or a driver? It's because they want you to feel like spending on these conveniences is completely natural and okay. They don't want you to think twice about how much you're actually spending because if you do, you will end up realizing just how expensive it's going to be. Sure, the occasional Uber or Lyft ride isn't so bad. But if you're constantly doing it every day on your daily commute, the bills will rack up. There are other alternatives to ride-hailing, like using a bike or carpooling with coworkers. These are much more sensible options that are also more financially sustainable.

Vacations

Vacations are always great. But it becomes problematic when you treat yourself to a vacation even when you don't have the funds for it. There are so many young people these days who force themselves to go on vacations because they see their friends on social media posting about their trips to the most lavish tourist destinations. So, in an effort to keep up with their friends, they'll try to force themselves into these trips as well. This is another classic example of letting your emotions control your spending. Yes, going on trips is great. But it's also expensive. You should only ever think about going on a vacation if you are financially secure enough to do so. Also, just because you can't afford to go on a vacation doesn't mean that you can't take a break from work. There are other more affordable alternatives to vacations that you can use to recharge and relax.

Entertainment

This includes concerts, music festivals, and movies. Again, it's important to remind you that it's not a bad thing to go see a concert of your favorite band or artist. It's not bad for you to want to watch the latest Marvel blockbuster on the big screen. These things in themselves aren't inherently bad. It's always nice to indulge in entertainment every once in a while. It's good for the soul. It's only bad when you're spending money that you don't have to indulge in these luxuries.

METHODS THAT CAN BE IMPLEMENTED TO CUT BACK ON UNNECESSARY SPENDING

It shouldn't come as a surprise to many that one of the most difficult aspects of financial management is cutting down on spending. Think about it. Whenever you ask a person what they think they should do in order to have more money at the end of the month, what's the first answer that would typically come to mind? They are likely to tell you that they need to get a higher income. Very rarely will you get someone who will answer that they need to cut back on their spending. This is because human beings are wired to come up with solutions in the form of addition as opposed to subtraction. In this case, people are more inclined to say that they just need more money to come in instead of saying that they need to keep more money from going out.

Understandably, it can be very tough to work within a budget, especially when you're young and you're not earning as much money. But this is why learning to lessen your spending is absolutely crucial. A lot of the time, you can only do so much when it comes to increasing your income. It can get to a point wherein your income is limited by your time and expertise. When that happens, the only solution you have left is to lessen your spending. To do this, you don't always have to start big. All it really takes to see a dramatic impact on your saving would be to lessen your spending in small but consistent ways.

. . .

Put Extra Money Into Savings Right Away

Doesn't it feel good whenever money just happens to fall into your lap unexpectedly? Maybe you find an extra hundred-dollar bill in a pair of jeans that you haven't worn in a while. Your boss at work might notice your hard work and give you a generous bonus. Maybe it's your birthday and your family members still make a habit of sending you money as a gift. Whatever the case, consider this kind of surprise cash as a bonus that you immediately need to put into your savings. Do not use these unexpected financial windfalls as a tool for you to spend more. Make it a habit for you to deposit that cash right away without spending it before it is all gone. That way, without cash on hand, you will not be tempted to spend on unnecessary things.

Always Cook Your Own Meals

Again, it can really be a hassle when you have to prepare every single meal you make. A lot of the time, you just want to get home after a tiring day at work to a fully cooked meal that's ready to eat. It can be really disheartening to get home feeling exhausted knowing that you have to make up a full meal from scratch. That can increase the temptation to just order takeout from somewhere instead. Resist that urge. There's an easy solution here and it's called meal preps. Essentially, just take one or two days out of the week to prepare all of your meals in bulk. Usually, people do this on Sundays and prepare a bunch of different meals for the whole week that you can just heat up whenever you're hungry. This is great because it helps you control your portions while also saving you the time and hassle of having to prepare a meal from scratch every time you have to eat.

. . .

Make a Grocery List and Stick to It

Too often, people will make the mistake of just mindlessly roaming around the grocery store without a proper list of items that they should buy. Again, when it comes to financial management, you must always be intentional with the way that you spend your money. Every purchase must serve some kind of purpose. This is why you should only buy grocery items that are actually a part of the plan. If you just roam around the grocery store in a lackadaisical fashion, then it becomes easier to buy things that you don't really need. By sitting down and writing out a grocery list, you can figure out what your absolute essentials are and it will prevent you from splurging on things that aren't necessary to your survival.

Set a Budget for Shopping

It's okay to go shopping even when you're trying to save money. Again, it's not about depriving yourself of life's pleasures. It's merely knowing how much money you have to spare for these pleasures. This is why you need to set a budget for yourself when it comes to your shopping. You must include the mandatory expenses as part of the budget. Even when you have some money leftover, it doesn't mean that you should blow it all in that month. Understand that you only have a certain amount of money to spend every month on simple pleasures and luxuries like clothes or gadgets. Stick to that budget. Also, if you don't have anything in particular that you want to buy for that month, then put your money into a shopping fund that you can pull from for bigger purchases in the future.

. . .

Sell Old Clothes to Fund New Ones

Another great way to cut back on spending when it comes to shopping is the art of selling things that you already have. In this example, we'll use clothes, but you can practically apply this technique to anything—even smaller items like books and old gadgets or bigger items like cars and furniture. Essentially, you need to sell off these older items to make way for newer ones. Take note that what you sell these older items off for isn't always going to be able to fully fund the newer purchase. But it can dramatically lessen what you would typically spend on that new item. Practicing this kind of habit will also prevent you from unnecessary hoarding.

Review Recurring Expenses

Even doing something as simple as sitting down to review all of your monthly recurring expenses will do a lot when it comes to saving your money. You just have to take a look at your recurring bills like subscriptions or memberships. Take the time to think about whether you really need these things. Sometimes, you don't even have to cancel these memberships or subscriptions altogether. You can also opt for downgrading your plans. It might seem like a very simple and obvious process, but it can do a lot for your savings, especially when you look at how much of your expenses you're cutting out over the course of a year.

Make Use of a Budget Tracker

Lastly, try to make use of a proper budget tracker. Some people will resort to using technological devices like smartphones. Of course, there are so many mobile apps available these days that will make financial tracking and management a lot easier. Every time you make a purchase, you just have to input it into your phone to make sure that the expense is logged. This will do two things for you. For one, it will make you think twice about a purchase before you actually go through with it. Second, it allows you to be organized and keep track of your overall expenses over the course of a week or a month. If you're not a fan of technology, then you can always go the traditional route by using a pen and paper. Just do whatever works best for you. The only important thing to keep in mind here is that you just need to keep track of your spending.

A PERSONAL STORY

In my old place of work, I remember coming across a 28-year-0ld girl. While working at our old company on a part-time basis, she was also a student. In order for her to get as much work done as she possibly could despite juggling a busy schedule, she conducted herself like a machine. Her daily routine mostly consisted of her getting to the office on time and immediately checking her emails. Then, at around 9AM, she would retreat from her desk to go somewhere and have a quick breakfast. On one of these occasions, she invited me to join her for breakfast. We went to her usual coffee shop and she had her customary bagel with cream cheese and medium French Vanilla coffee with some donuts. Her breakfast would typically round up to around $10. This was the kind of routine that she had indulged herself in consistently every day. She was always lamenting to me about how poor she was, but I didn't pay much mind to it. But one day, she actually showed me her bank account and I saw that she only had $5,000 in total assets to her name. This came as such a shock to me because I had a fairly good idea of how much she was making and how much she was spending at the time.

The $10 breakfast was only the tip of the iceberg for her. Usually, she skipped lunch because she wanted to *save money* but would only end up grabbing a snack some time in the afternoon. During her snack break, she would head to nearby convenience stores for a bag of chips and a drink. Sometimes, she also bought a chocolate bar or two. I was curious about her bank account and I saw how much money she was spending on food while at work. So, I decided to ask her a little bit more about her spending habits. She revealed to me that she also kept up a Spotify and Netflix Premium account that amounted to around $15 each. She also mentioned that she spent a lot of her money on maintaining her car along with other things. As she relayed all of this information to me, in my mind, all I could think about was how this was a person who needed to go on a spending diet. It also made me think about the many people in the same position as her who didn't even realize what they were doing wrong. The easy fix was right there staring at her in the face and she couldn't see it.

THE THIRD APPROACH: SAVING CHALLENGES

We briefly touched on the topic of prioritizing your savings over your expenses earlier. This is a piece of advice that you should definitely keep to heart. Before you even start laying out what your monthly budget is going to look like, it's important that you have a solid savings plan in place. When you start planning your budget, you might think that your monthly income is the war chest that you have to play with in order to map out your expenses. But that's not how it should work. Take your monthly income and automatically subtract your mandatory savings from it. Whatever is left behind is what you're supposed to be dedicating to your monthly expenses.

Hopefully, by now, you have a good grasp on why it's important to save your money. It doesn't matter how much money you're earning or how high your salary is. If you have poor saving habits, then you're just not going to achieve the kind of financial independence that you ultimately want. Granted, you might already understand why you need to have a proper savings scheme. But you still might not know how to go about it. The truth is that there are a myriad of ways to go about saving your money. It also depends on how much money you're taking in and what kind of lifestyle you lead. And if you're starting from scratch, you might not really know what your next steps might be. Don't worry. That's what this chapter is for.

This segment of the book is going to walk you through three specific savings schemes of varying deposit intervals and annual targets. Of course, while these savings schemes are very specific in its layout, you always have the power to amend or tweak them in whatever way you want so that it's more tailor-fitted to your needs and circumstances. At the end of the day, the only important thing here is that you establish a solid savings plan that you can stick to for the long-term. Staying consistent with a reliable savings plan is one of the best ways for you to reach and accomplish your financial goals in a timely fashion.

If you happen to be starting from scratch and you have zero savings in your bank account, then you can use this savings scheme as a way for you to build your emergency fund. The idea of an emergency fund is a concept that we've touched on multiple times throughout this book so far. There's really no understating just how important it is to have one. This is always the first goal that you need to prioritize whenever you're trying to set your finances straight. Once you have an emergency fund, you will have a lot more financial mobility and freedom. You would even find it easier to spend on luxuries once you have an emergency fund in place that you can fall back on. For now, if you're still building your emergency fund, then just purely focus on your savings. Avoid indulging in unnecessary splurges and expenses while you're still building that financial buffer. Even though it might take a lot of discipline and self-control to not participate in any unnecessary spending while you're building your fund, following a solid savings plan will help you stay on track and practice good habits.

365 DAYS SAVING METHOD

Again, your relationship with your finances has more to do with psychology than it does with anything else. That's why there is no sure-fire savings method that's going to work for everyone. It's a case-to-case basis and it's all dependent on personality types and dispositions. There are some people who prefer to carve out large chunks occasionally while there are others who are more predisposed to just saving a small amount consistently. One method isn't necessarily better than the other. Again, it's just a matter of finding the one that works best for you.

For this particular saving method, it's probably going to work best for the kind of people who want to just consistently add small amounts of money to a savings fund throughout the year. The whole concept is rooted in the idea that you pay yourself one penny on the first day of the year while adding one penny for each succeeding day. So, on the first day, you would pay one cent. On the second day, you would pay two cents. On the third day, three cents, and so on. By the end of the year, after following this method, you should have saved up as much as $667.95.

Of course, if that is how much your monthly income will allow for you to save, then that's fine. Work with what you have. But again, if you're capable of saving just a little bit more, then there's no problem with tweaking the savings plan just a bit to allow for you to save more money. Here's an example of how I tweaked the plan so that you would be able to save $16,699 by the end of the year.

By following this format, start a quarter or twenty-five cents on the first day. Then, double that amount to fifty cents on the next day. On the third day, double it again to a full dollar. Keep doubling the amount every day of the year and you'll eventually get to $16,699. Now, not everyone is capable of reaching this kind of money with their level of income and I understand that. But again, you're always free to tweak the plan however you see fit. This is mostly for people who think that it's best for them to keep on adding incremental amounts of money every day. And if this isn't your cup of tea, there are two other savings plans that you can try on for size.

52 WEEKS SAVING METHOD

If daily saving isn't really your thing, that's fine. It's understandable that you don't want to keep adding small amounts of money every single day into your savings fund. There are just some people who don't want to have to go through that process of transferring money every single day. That's okay. Perhaps, it would be better for you to take a weekly approach to adding to your savings. This 52-week saving scheme is a very simple and easy program that you can follow to end up with at least $1,378 by year's end. And it's a super simple formula to follow too! The way that this savings scheme works is that you start by adding one dollar to your fund in the first week of the year. Then, in the second week, you add two dollars. In the third week, add three dollars. Follow this pattern until the end of the year wherein you'll be adding $52 to your account on the final week. By the end, you will have an extra $1,378 in savings. It's a very easy program to follow because you would essentially just have to match a dollar for what week of the year it already is.

Again, if the amount of $1,378 is too easy or too difficult for you to achieve, there's no harm in changing things up. If you're incapable of doing it in the traditional way, then you can also choose to increase in increments of fifty cents as opposed to a full dollar every week. If the amount is too little for you, then you can do it in increments of two dollars per week instead. If you have a relatively higher income, you can really push yourself by working with $10 increments. So, instead of saving $1,378 dollars at the end of the year, you would have $13,780 dollars. The only draw with this kind of saving scheme is that it can get really difficult toward the end of the year and the numbers start getting really big. But if you stay committed, then you'll end up with a pretty hefty savings fund by the end.

26 WEEKS SAVING METHOD

This final saving scheme is mostly designed for those who would rather go on a biweekly schedule. It's a little less strenuous to maintain as you'll only have to add to your savings fund every couple of weeks or so. But it'll also demand bigger chunks of money from you in order for you to meet loftier savings goals. For people who are just starting out to save or have minimal income, you can use this savings scheme to actually save at least $1,000 by the end of the year. But if you have a little more wiggle room with your finances, you can always tweak the plan to your liking and financial capability.

The way that this savings plan works is that you merely have to divide $1,000 by 26, which would give you a quotient of 39. This means that you just have to put $39 into your savings account every two weeks and you'll end up with $1,000 after a full year. If you round your biweekly savings amount up to $40, then you'll end up with a total of $1,040 after 52 weeks. Again this amount might be a little too much or a little too low for you. It's okay for you to choose how much your biweekly output should be in order to account for your personal financial goals. Here's an example of a tweaked version of this savings scheme that would have you saving up $17,550 every year. To do this, aside from just having a standard amount that you put into your savings every two weeks, you add onto it.

Start with paying yourself $50 after the first two weeks. Then, you pay yourself $50 plus another $50 after the next couple of weeks. Take that amount and add another $50 two weeks after that. Keep on adding $50 to the amount that you put into your savings every two weeks and you'll end up with $17,550 by the end of the year.

HOW MUCH MONEY SHOULD YOU REALLY SAVE?

Now, you already have a good grasp on some standard savings schemes that you can use to force yourself to save more money. You can merely choose the one that you think best suits your personality type. It doesn't really matter what kind of mechanism or format you follow. The only important thing here is you find one that best helps you meet your goals. However, you might still be wondering about how much money you should be really saving at the end of each month or year. That's a valid thing to really think about. How do you know when you're saving too little or too much? After all, even if you have the proper savings plan in place, it's not really going to help much if you're not setting the right savings goals.

The difficult thing is that there really aren't any written rules about how much money you should be saving every month or year. It differs based on specific financial situations and circumstances. However, a good rule of thumb that you should always shoot for is around 20% of your monthly income. So, if you earn $5,000 a month, then you should try to save $1,000 of it. And of that $1,000, dedicate half of it to your retirement fund or other investments while the other half goes to building your emergency funds. This is money that you need to force yourself to set aside every month and never spend unless absolutely necessary.

Again, this is just a soft suggestion for how much of your money you should be saving every month or year. If you feel like you're capable of saving more money, then go ahead. If you have debts to pay off, then maybe you can dedicate 10% of your income to savings and the other 10% toward paying off your debt. This way, you have a more structured way of still building your savings fund while also paying off those pesky debts that are keeping you in a financial hole. Stick to a proper system religiously and you will find that your financial situation is going to get significantly better over time.

Also, keep in mind that saving is only one part of being financially responsible. You also have to pay attention to your investments and your expenses. But that's okay. In the next chapter, we will be taking a more holistic approach to the management of your finances by discussing your cash flow.

A PERSONAL STORY

One time, I was engaged in a conversation with a work colleague about savings and finances. I tried my best to stifle my shock and emotions when I heard how much he managed to save over the course of a year. At that point, I was very much aware of how much he was earning and so I had a good sense of how much money he should have been saving. That's why it took every ounce of my energy to try and comprehend why he only managed to save $520 over the course of the year! Of course, I understand that $520 is a lot of money for a lot of people and it might be the best that many can do given their circumstances. I fully understand that. But again, I knew this person and I knew how much money they were taking home every month. There was no valid reason for them to only be saving $520 over the course of a year.

Apparently, he only got to that amount because he set up an auto transfer system from his checking account to his savings every week. By transferring $10 on a weekly basis to his savings, he managed to save just $520 in a year. Again, to many people this is the best that they can do and that's fine. But I knew that this guy was earning a paycheck that was significantly much higher than that amount and it bugged me every time he started complaining about how little he was saving. He also started talking about how he wished that he was born into a wealthy family and a life of privilege like other people have been. We worked in the company together for around three years and I knew that he managed to grow his total assets from $1,000 to $5,000 dollars within that span thanks to tax refunds and his $520 annual savings. To me, that was just a lot of failed potential. He might have just been *getting by*, but he could have been doing so much more with just a little extra effort and proper direction. I don't know where he is now and I hope that he gets a chance to read this book.

THE FOURTH APPROACH: MONEY HERE, MONEY THERE

As boring as it might sound, the process of managing your personal cash flow is very important. There are too many people out there who go month by month without paying close attention to how their money is moving both into and out of their lives. How many times have you taken a look at your bank account at the end of the month only to realize that you don't have as much money as you thought? After you pay off your utilities and credit card bills, you discover that you don't have enough money left over for other things. Heck, you might even find your total assets diminishing over time without realizing why.

In order for you to avoid finding yourself in such a situation, it's important that you take the time to really account for the inflow and outflow of your cash. This means that you have to conduct simple accounting for your income (ideally, you have more than one stream of income) and your expenses. Try producing financial statements at the end of every month. These will essentially serve as comprehensive reports detailing your current financial condition. You might think that only businesses and companies should concern themselves with such matters. But that's a mistake. The reason that businesses become successful is because they pay attention to all of the financial details. There should be no reason why you should be doing any different.

For the penultimate approach to achieving financial independence, we are going to talk about how you can establish better control over the movement of your money. In this chapter, we will go over such concepts like cash flow analysis, budget tracking, and mild investing. Ultimately, this chapter will serve as a great blueprint for how you can really track the way your money moves, and by extension, the way you behave in a financial sense. Knowledge of such mechanisms will allow you to better pinpoint holes or weaknesses in your financial routine so that you can improve them to boost your financial situation.

PERSONAL CASH FLOW ANALYSIS

Cash flow analysis or management is essentially the process of understanding the sources of your income, the extents of your expenses, and how you are utilizing your cash to achieve certain financial goals. Many money experts will tell you that cash flow analysis is one of the most important aspects of achieving genuine financial success and independence. Again, it's not just a matter of securing a job that manages to pay you well. Having a sizable income certainly matters, but it's not the whole story. That's only one aspect of your cash flow. It's imperative that you take a deeper understanding of the many facets of your personal cash flow.

. . .

How Do You Analyze Your Cash Flow?

The first step to analyzing your cash flow starts with determining all your sources of income. Ideally, you would have as many streams of income as you can possibly handle. Most people are content with merely having their basic salaries from their nine to five jobs as their only source of income. That would be a mistake. Again, if you want to achieve financial independence in the future, you should definitely keep your nine to five for now. But that doesn't mean that it should be the only thing that you're living off of. Try diversifying your inflow of cash by generating more income streams. Here are a few common examples of different kinds of income:

1. **Earned Income:** Again, this is the most basic and common type of income for a lot of people. For most of the working population, this also tends to be the source of income that yields the biggest amount. Stick with your day job and maximize the financial benefits of your employment as much as possible. But don't be content with just settling for this income stream only.
2. **Profit Income:** This kind of income is generated whenever you are able to sell something at a price higher than what it cost you to procure it. Profit can either come in the form of a tangible object like a piece of merchandise or a service. Usually, you can generate profit income by starting your own business. For example, you can have a meal preparation service. You can charge customers a price that's higher than what it cost you to procure and prepare their meals for them. The margins that you establish in your sales will serve as your profits.

3. **Dividends Income:** Dividends are essentially cash rewards that are dealt out by companies toward its shareholders. However, it's important to note that not all companies practice regular dividend distribution. For the most part, big companies will offer annual or quarterly dividend distribution toward their shareholders depending on how well their businesses have performed. You can be entitled to dividends by buying shares of a company through the stock market.
4. **Rental Income:** As its name implies, rental income is any kind of money that you can get as a result of renting or leasing out an item that you own. This can come in the form of land or equipment. For example, you can get rental income by leasing out an apartment or a house to prospective renters. But you can also get rental income by renting out equipment like cars, audio equipment, and the like. You can only get this kind of income if you have ownership over a certain commodity that others would be willing to rent for money.
5. **Capital Gains:** The last kind of income that we'll be talking about today is capital gains. Essentially, you can get capital gains by selling something at a higher value than when you initially bought it. For example, you can buy stocks from Apple that are valued at $100. Over the course of a year, that stock might rise to $150 in value. If you sell all of your stocks, you will gain an income of $50 in the form of capital gains. This can also work for other items that increase in value over time like property, luxury watches, art, and more.

To put it simply, your cash inflow is any money that comes into your life. When you're making your cash flow analysis, identify how much money is coming in and where it's coming from. For example, you might have $5,000 coming from your earned income or monthly salary. Then, in a certain month, you might have managed to cash out on a sale of a stock that earned you a profit of $100 in capital gains. If a company that you have shares in decides to give dividends, take note of that too. Take all of these sources of income and consolidate them. This will serve as your total cash inflow.

After that, you need to identify where your cash is going. This is where you need to start listing down all of your expenses and categorizing them appropriately so that they are organized. Of course, not everyone's cash flow analysis statements are going to look the same. We all have different sources of income and we spend our money on different things. So, don't worry about being so strict about how you're supposed to format your expenses. However, if you're looking for a guide, there are typically five types of expenses that most people tend to flow their money through.

1. **Rent or Mortgage:** If you're renting or if you're paying for your mortgage, then you should classify this as your residence or living expense. This includes all of the money that you're paying on rent, association dues, or mortgage payments.
2. **Utilities:** Your utilities are essentially everything that you need to maintain the functionality of your home. This includes expenses like electricity, telecommunications, water, and the like.
3. **Transportation:** Regardless if you're a car owner or not, you need to take note of how much money you're spending on transportation over the course of

the month. This includes the money that you spend on gasoline or parking fees. If you don't own a car, calculate how much money you spend on train or bus rides.
4. **Groceries:** Of course, you need to account for your groceries as well. The food that you buy to stock up your home's pantry is an expense that a lot of people tend to not pay attention to.
5. **Entertainment:** Now, you also need to take note of all your expenses on things that are for entertainment. This includes subscription services like Netflix or Spotify. But this can also cover other forms of recreation like books, movie tickets, dinners out, and more.

The whole point of determining your cash flow is simple: it's to make sure that you aren't spending more money than you're earning. Subtract your total expenses from your total income and that will give you your net cash flow. If you're in the positive, then that's good. If you're in the negative, then that's obviously bad and you need to make a change. But it's not enough that you have a positive net cash flow. The goal is to make that number as big as possible without compromising the quality of your life too dramatically. Of course, it's not wise to just spend all of your time increasing your cash inflow at the expense of your health and personal well-being. It also isn't good to deprive yourself of life's pleasures just because you're too guilty about spending on such things. Again, you just have to strike that proper balance. Everything in moderation.

Make a Personal Balance Sheet

Another aspect of analyzing your cash flow is the personal balance sheet. To put it simply, a balance sheet gives you a good screenshot of what your general financial situation looks like at any given moment. Having a balance sheet is important because it gives you a gauge of whether your cash flow has been good or bad. As you analyze your balance sheets over extended periods, you'll get to know whether you're progressing or regressing in your financial journey. A balance sheet is essentially composed of a summary of everything that you own (assets), everything that you owe (liability), and your total financial worth (net worth).

Assets

As previously mentioned, an asset is anything that you own. So, any item that is legally and rightfully within your possession that has quantifiable value is a financial asset. There are three categories of assets that you need to take note of. The first is a liquid asset. Liquid assets are the items that are within your possession and have immediate access to while also carrying a certain monetary value. So, this includes the cold hard cash in your savings accounts, money market accounts, and the cash in your wallet. Then, there are large assets. These are the items that you own which also carry a certain monetary value, but aren't as easily convertible to a cash amount. Examples of large assets include houses, cars, jewelry, boats, furniture, and artwork. When you're discerning the value of large assets, make sure that you account for its market value and not its retail value. In other words, account for how much you can sell it for and not how much you bought it for. Your selling price can be either higher or lower than your buying price. Lastly, there are your other assets which are less tangible in nature but remain assets nonetheless. These include investments in bonds, stocks, mutual funds, and real estate.

Liabilities

Liabilities are what you would find on the opposite side of a balance sheet. They are essentially any amount of money that you owe to other people or institutions. To put it simply, they are debts that you haven't paid. This can include mortgages, unpaid bills, business loans, car loans, and student loans.

Net Worth

Your net worth is basically your total worth in financial terms. While you should never define yourself in terms of just finances, it's important that you develop a total awareness of your net worth. This is because knowing your net worth will give you a good idea of what your financial health is and whether you're close to reaching your financial goals or not. Your net worth shouldn't be seen as the definition of your character. Rather, it's a tool that you can use to measure your progress in your financial journey.

To calculate your net worth, you essentially have to subtract all of your liabilities from your total assets. If you come out on the positive side, then that's great. You should focus on continually building your financial war chest. If your liabilities outnumber your assets, then your number one priority would be to pay down your debt while also building your emergency fund.

THE BASIC RULES OF BUDGETING

For this part of the book, we're going to talk about how you can develop a budget system for yourself. If you've never tried conscious and intentional budgeting before, don't worry. It might seem really intimidating at first, but this part of the book is going to hold your hand and walk you through every step of the process from the beginning.

The very first thing that you need to do is to track your expenses over the course of 30 days. When you're tracking, take note of the amount of every transaction and who you're paying the amount to. For example, $30 to the barber, $120 to the grocery store, $50 to the telephone company, etc. It doesn't matter how big or how small these transactions are. You have to take note of them right down to the last cent. And again, it's important that you also take note of where this money is going. These two details are absolutely crucial in developing your budget plan.

Even in this initial phase of the budgeting process, you are going to go through a certain kind of enlightenment when it comes to your finances. This is especially true if you've never done budgeting before. You will become more conscious over just how much money you waste on senseless things. And don't be ashamed. Everyone is guilty of that to a certain extent. Be proud that you're now starting to take better control over your spending. You would be surprised at where your money is really going versus where you think is going. That's why this step of the process is so important.

Then, after you take note of your expenses, it's time to track your income. If you only have one source of income so far, then that means it will be relatively easy for you to track. However, again, you should always work at trying to diversify your income streams if you want to eventually achieve financial independence. If you already have multiple streams of income, then that's good. Do the same process as you did with your expenses. Document how much money is coming in and where it's coming from over the course of 30 days.

The next step is for you to add everything up. Total all of your expenses and all of your income. Ideally, you're earning more than you're spending. If you are, then you're already on the right track. If not, then you need to make a serious adjustment to the way that you handle your budget. Regardless, everything that you've done so far is going to give you the info that you need to develop a proper budget plan for yourself.

Now, before we move on to the next phase of budgeting, it's important to emphasize that there are a myriad of different ways in which people budget their money. There is no absolute one way of budgeting that rules all. Again, it's all a matter of finding a system that fits and works best for you. You can always work your own budget plan that you devise by yourself, but there's no shame in adopting a budget plan from someone else either. For the purposes of this book, we will be talking about the **50/30/20** rule that was popularized by American politician Elizabeth Warren. It's a very popular budget plan because of its simplicity and practicality.

The whole premise of the plan is for you to create a budget that caters to three specific things: your needs, wants, and financial goals. Your needs should basically be composed of the absolute necessary expenses like rent, groceries, and utility bills like electricity, internet, and water. Your wants are made up of the things that give you pleasure in life like vacations, dinners out, hobbies, nice clothes, toys, gadgets, subscriptions, and others. Lastly, there are your financial goals. Your financial goals can be made up of your emergency fund, retirement fund, debt payments, insurance payments, and investments. To identify these things correctly, take some time to categorize all of your expenses into these three classifications. If necessary, refer to the list of expenses that you made over 30 days. After that, take your total income amount and allocate your money appropriately. Fifty percent of your income should go to funding your needs. Thirty percent should go to funding the things that you want. Twenty percent should go to serving your financial goals. So, let's assume that you have a monthly take-home pay of $10,000. This is how your budget should look:

Total Income: $10,000

$5,000 should be allocated for electricity bills, groceries, rent, etc.

$3,000 should go to shopping, dinners out, subscriptions, vacation funds, etc.

$2,000 should go to stock market investments, retirement funds, insurance plans, etc.

It's really as simple as that. If you're a novice at budgeting, it's fairly easy to see why this plan is so appealing. It's incredibly easy to grasp and execute. It also tends to be very sustainable and applicable for a wide variety of people. The 50/30/20 plan works for a variety of different personality types and income brackets.

Now, there are other important things that you need to remember here. First, you don't always have to spend all of the money that you allocate for a specific expense. For example, if you notice at the end of the month that you've only spent $2,500 on your wants, that doesn't mean you have to force yourself to spend the remaining $500. You should divert any of your surpluses to your financial goals instead.

Another thing you want to really iron out are the expenses that can fall into multiple categories. For example, groceries are typically considered as *needs*. However, while you're in the grocery store, you can also purchase items that you don't need such as junk food or alcohol. These are items that should fall under the *want* category and you should take note of these discrepancies accordingly. Generally, if it's not crucial to your functionality and survival, it should be considered as a want.

Also, the 50/30/20 plan might not work out so well for low-income individuals who might also be dealing with large amounts of debt. That extra 20% that should go toward funding financial goals are often utilized to cover basic needs. Not everyone has the luxury of allocating 20% of their monthly income to invest in the stock market or build an emergency fund. That's just a sad reality for many people who are struggling with their income.

If you feel like the 50/30/20 plan just isn't for you, then there are alternatives that you can try out as well. There is the 80/20 rule which takes a more relaxed and lenient approach to budgeting. With the 80/20 rule, you would have to just automatically set aside 20% of your income toward your savings or financial goals. Then, you can do whatever you want with the rest of your money. There is also the 70/20/10 rule which is mostly targeted toward people who are in debt. In this budgeting format, you would have to dedicate 70% of your income to living expenses, 20% to debt payments, and 10% to your savings.

DEALING WITH DEBT

It's obvious that if you're dealing with debt, the path toward financial independence becomes a lot more complicated. You're not just starting from scratch at this point. You're starting at a deficit. So, the art of saving and budgeting become a lot more challenging for you. However, that shouldn't deter you from trying to better your situation. It doesn't matter if your debt is big or small. The sooner you start trying to resolve your debt, the better. The longer you put it off, the more difficult you would be making it for yourself in the future. If you're still paying off certain debts, then you need to keep in mind the following principles:

Be Aware of How Much Debt You Have

The first thing that you need to do to solve this problem, as it is with any problem, is to know just what it is you're up against. Sit down and make a list of all of your debts. Identify who you owe money to and how much you owe each of them. Also make sure that you note the corresponding interest rates for each particular debt. This might be an incredibly uncomfortable process as it forces you to come to terms with the reality of your situation, but it's a necessary one. You must be willing to acknowledge the gravity of the problem in order for you to resolve it.

Once you've written this list out, make sure that you keep it handy and accessible at all times. You want to be able to access it as you progress toward eliminating each debt one by one until you're in the green. Some experts say that it would be useful for you to calculate for your Debt to Income Ratio or DTI. To do this, you need to take your monthly debt payment and divide it by your monthly income. Let's assume that you have a monthly income of $5,000 and you've found out that your monthly debt payments amount to around $2,000.

DTI = 2,000 / 5,000 = 0.4 * 100 = 40%

This means that your monthly debt payments amount to 40% of your monthly income. That's how much money you need to set aside every month in order for you to pay off your debts on time. Ideally, you have a low DTI ratio. The lower the number, the smaller your problem.

Make Payments on Time

Another key principle to getting out of debt is making sure that you make payments on time. As much as possible, you don't want to add to your debts by allowing late fees and penalties. That'll just prolong the debt payment process and it will make it harder for you to eventually climb out of that financial hole. It's essential that you try to complete full payments every month as much as possible. If your income is high enough to cover your monthly debt payments, then that's great. Make sure that you set aside enough cash to cover these expenses even if it means that you have to temporarily compromise the quality of your lifestyle for a while. Cut down on your unnecessary expenses and don't put too much of your money into your savings. Focus on the debt first and once that is cleared, everything else becomes easier.

Know Your Options

When it comes to addressing your debts, there are several routes you can take and they all depend on your financial situation. They all come with their own sets of pros and cons and it's best for you to really discern which one would be most beneficial to your situation.

Avalanche Method

The Avalanche Method in debt payment is a top-down approach to resolving your debt. Essentially, the method works by first addressing the debt with the highest interest rates. Since these debts tend to cost you more money over longer periods of time, then it makes more sense to address them right away so that it's easier to tackle the other debts. To do this method, you just have to follow these steps:

1. Choose the debt that has the highest interest rates and put as much money as you can toward paying that debt off every month.
2. Make just minimum payments on every other debt that you have.
3. Continue this process until that highest debt is paid off.
4. Repeat the process with the next high-interest debt account until all your debts are paid.

Snowball Method

The Snowball Method is the opposite of the Avalanche Method wherein instead of a top-down approach, you would be dealing with the smallest and littlest debts first. So, the reason why someone would want to use the Snowball Method is for instant success and gratification. One of the cons of using the Avalanche Method is that it can take quite a while for some people to pay off their highest and most difficult debts. By using the Snowball Method, you get success much more quickly because you're dealing with the easiest ones first. This success can serve as a great motivator to just keep on pushing until all of the debt is just eliminated altogether. Here is how you can go about the Snowball Method:

1. List down all of your debts and rank them from the easiest to resolve to the hardest.
2. Devote most of your funds towards paying off the easiest debt first.
3. Make minimum payments on the other debts every month.
4. Once the first debt is paid off, move down the list and keep on repeating the process until all debts are resolved.

Debt Consolidation

For most people, they get into serious debt problems because they have debts coming in from everywhere—student loans, mortgages, car loans, credit card debts. The list can go on and on. Having to deal with so many different kinds of debts can be quite exhausting and overwhelming. On top of that, they can have varying interest rates, which can further complicate an already challenging predicament. This is where debt consolidation can come in as a handy solution. Essentially, the way that debt consolidation works is that you would take out a loan from somewhere (whether it be a friend or a reputable financial institution) and use that loan to pay off all of your other debts. That way, you consolidate all of your debt categories into a single loan that you can dedicate all of your focus and energy toward resolving.

If you choose to go this route, make sure that you try to seek out loans with relatively reasonable interest rates. Sometimes, you might be subjecting yourself to a loan with an outrageously high interest rate that will leave you paying so much more than you have to. Do all of the necessary calculations beforehand and if the math checks out, then this can always serve as a viable option.

Debt Settlement

Another route that you can choose to go with is the debt settlement strategy. The thing that you have to understand about lenders is that they want you to be able to pay your debts back. As much as possible, they need to get that money back from you. You might think that a lot of them are evil and selfish financial institutions who are trying to take advantage of your unfortunate financial situation. But you would be surprised at how willing they would be to help you out with your problems. That's why debt settlement is something that you should always consider.

Essentially, debt settlement is when you go to your lender and you try to negotiate an adjustment of your debt terms. At the very least, you can try to ask your lender if they would be willing to ease up on your penalty fees or interest rates so that it becomes easier for you to pay your debts off in full. There are even sometimes wherein lenders will just forgive the debt altogether if the circumstances are right. However, you should know that this is a long shot and it isn't always going to work. But if you're in a deep financial bind and you've got nothing else to lose, then it doesn't hurt to try.

To execute a proper debt settlement, you can either just go straight to the lender or work with a third-party debt settlement company. There are pros and cons to both approaches. If you just go through the entire process yourself, there's a lot of preparatory work that you need to do in order to really prove that they need to consider making it easier for you to pay your debts off. Sometimes, this process can get really drawn out and you're going to have to go through the stresses of the back-and-forths between you and the lender. However, you can also hire a debt settlement company. With this approach, the company will handle all of the stressful aspects for you. But it's going to cost you money. And if you're in a deep financial bind already because of your debts, this isn't always feasible.

Bankruptcy

The last option that you have, and hopefully it never comes to this, is bankruptcy. This should always be your last resort because while the prospect of a fresh start might sound really tempting, it can also make it harder for you to take on healthy debts in the future. It's really going to tarnish your credit score and that might make it difficult for you to take out loans for homes, businesses, or other potential assets in the future. Also, bankruptcy is not as easy and as clean-cut as you might think. You're going to have to hire an attorney and you will have to shell out some cash to carry out the process. Ironically enough, there are some people out there who are so broke that they can't even afford to process their bankruptcy.

A PERSONAL STORY

I had a friend who bought a car worth around $20,000. She was able to save a little bit of money at that time, so she thought she was able to afford the car. I also knew that she had a monthly income of around $3,000. And that's why I was taken aback when we started talking about her finances and I discovered that her fixed and variable expenses amounted to roughly around $3,500 on a monthly basis. This was quite alarming to me because she was consistently spending more than she earned. It doesn't take a rocket scientist to figure out that given enough time, you'll eventually run out of money if you keep spending more than you're earning.

Moreover, the only reason that she was consistently spending more than she was earning was because she wasn't making any efforts to keep track of her cash flow. She only had rough estimates of how much money was coming in and how much she was spending. But she never really made any conscious efforts to know and control the movement of her money. At the end of every billing cycle, she found herself struggling to pay off her credit card bills while also worrying about her mounting debt. I wasn't surprised that she was going through such challenges because she had poor financial habits. Given that she was my friend, I wanted to help her out. I sat down with her and created an Excel tracking sheet for her income and expenditures. After sitting down and going through all of her finances, I saw that there was an easy fix to her problem. She just needed to cut down on her transportation and dining expenses, and she would be in good financial shape. She also had a habit of eating out a lot and it was taking a huge chunk out of her budget.

I explained to her what she had to do but she still showed no signs of willingness to change. She didn't want to give up her car even though I told her that the gasoline and maintenance costs were too much. It made much more sense to just take public transportation. Maybe it was pride or something else.

But she was adamant about not giving up the car. I also told her to cut down on eating out because she could have saved so much more money by just preparing her own food. Again, she wasn't convinced and she justified her dining out as a necessary expense. She said that she didn't have the time or patience to go grocery shopping and prepare her own food. I was disappointed to hear this from her, but I didn't force the issue. I still wished her the best, but in the end, she ended up having to move back into her parents' place while still keeping her car.

THE FIFTH APPROACH: CUT DOWN ON AVOIDABLE EXPENSES

*T*rim the fat. Try to adopt as financially lean a lifestyle as possible. We already talked about how you can cut back on unnecessary spending in an earlier chapter. But to end this book, we're going to take an even deeper dive into your expenses. More specifically, we're going to look at some of the common expenses that you should always look to avoid having, especially when you're still in the process of trying to build your personal wealth. To repeat, expenses are tricky to deal with because it's not always the first target for people who are looking to build their wealth.

There is a popular social experiment in which people are given five identical Lego block pieces. Three of these five pieces are stacked onto one side and the other two pieces are stacked on another side. Then, the participants of the experiment are handed another Lego piece that can connect both stacks. However, since the stacks are uneven, it's difficult for people to make a solid connection with the extra piece. When asked what the most obvious solution is, most people would say that they need to add another block of Lego to the stack of two in order to make it even with the other stack. That's always the most intuitive thing to do. Very few will come up with the solution to take away one block from the stack of three even though it is also a valid solution. Instinctively, people are just inherently wired to solve a problem by addition instead of subtraction. This is a phenomenon that is consistent with various aspects of life, even finance.

When you ask someone how they can be rich, their common instinct is always to say that they need to add more money to their bank account. However, very few people will say that they need to subtract from their expenses, even though it can also produce an equally valid solution to the problem. There are always two sides to the solution. And yes, it's always good to try to increase your income. But there's no reason that you shouldn't be making any efforts to subtract from your expenses as well. That's something that we'll try to address together in this final chapter of the book.

WHY YOU NEED TO CUT BACK ON YOUR EXPENSES

Spending in itself is not an inherently bad habit. It's only bad when people overindulge in it. It's the same as a slice of chocolate cake or a juicy cheeseburger. It's okay to indulge in these things every once in a while. They're not going to make a significant difference on your overall health if you eat this kind of food in moderation. But if you're consistently eating junk, then that's when it becomes a problem. It's the same with spending. You always have the right to spend, but it's not a right that you want to abuse if you're concerned about your financial health.

If you're a bit of a *spendaholic*, then you may have difficulty coming to terms with the fact that you need to make a change in life. And that's okay. Change doesn't always come naturally. But in order to expedite the process, here are a few reasons that might be able to motivate you to really adopt new ways of handling your money.

You Focus on Quality Over Quantity

When you are mindful about cutting back on your expenses, you start to second-guess your purchases. You know that you only have a limited budget to work with and you can't be reckless when it comes to spending your money. So, you force yourself to really buy things that you can maximize. Instead of spending a lot of your cash on unnecessary items that you need to replace over and over again, you will end up doing a lot more research to find things that will last you a long time. This way, you get the most bang for your buck.

A lot of people who are budget-conscious will really take their time to think about their purchases before actually going through them. So, when you're strolling along in the mall and you find a pair of boots that you really like, take a pause. Think about it for a while. At that moment, you might think that you need it and that you can afford it. But don't do anything. Go back home and really think about whether you need those boots. A lot of the time, you will end up talking yourself out of the purchase because you will realize that it isn't necessary after all. But if you're still obsessing over it after a couple of weeks, then make sure that you have enough money in your budget that will allow for you to buy it. Otherwise, save up for it first and then come back to buy it.

. . .

You Develop Your Self-Awareness

Not a lot of people realize this but their spending habits tend to correlate with the state of their mental health. This is where the very idea of *retail therapy* comes from. There are just certain people who get a kick out of making purchases even when they're totally unnecessary or unreasonable. The sheer act of buying something is enough to make them feel good about themselves and that's a very unhealthy way to approach handling finances. If you are conscious about the way you spend, it might reveal certain aspects about your personality and the state of your mental health that were previously hidden to you.

Of course, there is no shame in admitting that you might have a tendency to tie your sense of self-worth to how much money you have or the things that you buy. It's only a shame if you refuse to see that it's a problem and you don't take any measures to address the problem. By addressing certain issues that you're dealing with mentally, you may also be attacking the root of a bunch of other compounding problems that you have in your life.

It's Good for Your Mental Health

In connection with the previously listed item, being more budget-conscious is just going to benefit your mental health. We've already talked about the damaging properties of financial stress that many people have to go through when they're undergoing money problems. A lot of the stress that comes with money problems comes from feeling like you don't have any control over your life. But what most people in dire financial situations don't realize is that they always have control. If you become more conscious about the way you spend, you establish more of that control over your finances and you will realize that this is a problem that you can solve after all.

When you cut back on your expenses, you will help revitalize your financial health and this is going to do wonders for your mental health, by extension. You also save yourself from falling into bad financial habits and situations. You can help stifle the formation of any harmful routines that could potentially impact your mental health in a negative manner.

You Get More Financial Mobility

And lastly, you gain more financial mobility. By being more conscious about your spending, you are keeping more of your money with you. You can dedicate more of your hard-earned cash toward things that can actually serve you and add value to your life. Instead of splurging on a pair of designer shoes that you don't really need, you will have the freedom to invest that money into stocks and other money-earning vehicles that will help grow your cash for you. Instead of splurging on a lavish vacation, you can put your money toward a retirement fund that will serve you well in the future.

However, it's important to note that total deprivation of happiness and recreation is not the goal here. Again, it's all about moderation. If you have the capacity to spend on things that give you joy, then that's fine. It's just important to make sure that you are doing so responsibly. It will feel a lot better when you can buy a nice luxury bag for yourself knowing that you still have a lot of money in the bank that can cover your basic needs and any potential emergencies.

BEFORE SPENDING, ASK YOURSELF THESE FIVE THINGS

Sticking to a budget is no easy feat. That's a universal truth that applies to everyone. This is especially true if you have such a tight budget to work with and you've grown accustomed to a certain lifestyle that demands so much of your finances. The truth is that a lot of budgeting has to do with priorities. Do you prioritize taking that vacation to Europe now or should you be investing in a college fund for your kids? Do you buy that dream car that you've always wanted or should you put your money in stocks instead? Should you take out a higher loan for that nicer place in the city or should you go for a more modest suburban home? Ultimately, the answers to these questions lie in what your priorities are. But how do you ultimately decide what you should prioritize?

It's a constant battle between what you want and what you need. It's a battle between your logic and emotions. It's a battle between delayed gratification or instant satisfaction. Again, finance has a lot to do with psychology. Money can affect our decision making from small purchases like gum at the register area to big things like accepting a bribe for something.

Whenever you're feeling the urge to spend, then there are certain psychological hacks that you can employ to make sure that you're making the right choice when it comes to your finances. If you're still trying to develop your instincts for spending and are unsure of how you should be making your decisions, don't worry. You just need to sharpen your introspection. To do so, try to implement the habit of asking yourself the following questions, especially before making big purchases.

Do You Really Need It?

This is always the first thing that you need to ask yourself prior to making any kind of purchase. For the most part, if you decide that you need it, then it's a lot easier to justify the expense. But if you come to the realization that you don't need it, then you have to continue to justify the expense in other ways and that isn't going to be easy. In fact, a lot of the time, people can just stop with this one question and it would be enough to deter them from making any unnecessary purchases.

But not every purchase you make should be for something you need. It's okay for you to indulge in a few *irresponsible* or *irrational* purchases every once in a while. That's ultimately why you want to work your way toward decent financial health. Having a huge chunk of savings in the bank will give you more financial freedom to partake in these indulgences. But if you're still in the process of building your finances, just stick to what you need for the most part. It's about doing what you have to do now so that you can enjoy the fruits of your labor later on.

What Value Does It Bring to Your Life?

The next question you need to ask yourself is what kind of value or impact the purchase will have on your life. Earlier, we talked about how you should be prioritizing only the things that you need. Obviously, if it's a genuine *need* like food, water, shelter, or clothing, then it offers a lot of value to your life. These are things that you can't live without. But if you don't *need* a certain purchase, then you can try to justify it by thinking about what kind of value it can bring to your life.

For example, many people might argue that you don't need a high-speed internet connection. However, in your case, you might use that high-speed internet to help you work on your side hustles. Maybe you have a job on the side that earns you money and requires a high-speed internet connection for you to be successful at it. In that case, spending on a high-speed internet plan might prove to be very valuable to you. Therefore, it's an expense that makes sense.

But aside from that, asking yourself this question can also force you to get rid of expenses that you're constantly paying even though they don't bring much value to you. This includes junk food, alcohol, subscription services, and other usual suspects.

Are There Cheaper Alternatives?

Never underestimate the value of getting the better deal. There are various utilities that you might think that you need in life like cars, computers, smartphones, and others. The beauty of modern-day consumerism is that there is no shortage of options on the market for you to choose from. Whenever you're tempted to buy something and you've somehow justified to yourself that it's a purchase you need to make, then that's fine. But don't be so close-minded. Consider other alternatives to that particular item, especially if there are cheaper ones.

For example, if you're convinced that you need to invest in new suits to wear to your office, then that's okay. After all, your job is what is going to give you the income to sustain yourself. Buying new suits might be seen as an investment. But that doesn't mean that you have to go for brands like Tom Ford or Brooks Brothers right away, especially if you're on a budget. There are various tailors out there who would be able to provide you with perfectly adequate suits at more reasonable rates. This is a much more pragmatic option than splurging on a designer suit.

But there is also a caveat to this. Cheaper doesn't always mean better. Sometimes, if you're trying to cut costs too much, then you end up compromising a lot of that quality. Then, you might end up finding yourself having to replace that item more frequently because of the substandard quality. This will have you spending more money in the long run than if you just bought a more premium item on the first go. For instance, you have a choice of buying a $3,000 car manufactured in 2001 or $9,000 car manufactured in 2011. Yes, at first sight you should go for the cheaper car, but when you think about it, the cheaper car is really old and might require a lot of maintenance and fixing. So, for the long run, it would be a better choice for you to spend more for a newer model that requires less maintenance. Do your research. Get the option that brings the most bang out of your buck.

Can You Really Afford It Now?

The next question that you need to ask is whether you can really afford the purchase right now. If you can, then it makes the decision a lot easier. If you're splurging on a luxury item that you don't really need, then here's a good rule of thumb to keep in mind: if you can't afford to buy four of it in one go, then you can't afford it at all. Just stay patient and continue to save your money until you have enough in the bank to be able to really afford it. If it's the kind of purchase that you have to take a loan out for like a car or a house, things can get even more complicated. You really have to study the loan properly and make sure that you have the capacity to never miss payments without having to dip into your emergency savings. If you're confident that you can do so, then that's an acceptable purchase.

Will You End up Saving More Money by Spending Now?

The last thing that you have to ask yourself is whether it makes sense for you to spend a little more money now so that you end up saving money in the future. For example, picture a scenario where you're in the market for a car. You're at the used car dealership and you're trying to get the best deal that you can. The car dealer tells you that there's a 2011 Toyota Camry on the lot that costs just $8,000. But he also tells you that there's a 2016 Toyota Camry on the lot that costs $17,000. It's more than double the amount. Naturally, you might think that going for the 2011 version is the more financially responsible option.

However, the more you think about it, you discover that you'll have to put the car through a lot more maintenance processes because it's an older model. You also know that it won't have as long a lifespan of the newer model and you might end up having to replace it a lot earlier. Then, in your mind, when you start doing the computations, you might come to the realization that you'll end up spending more in the long run if you go for the cheaper option now. In that sense, it's much better for you to just splurge on the more expensive model now so that you will end up saving more in the future.

FIXED EXPENSE VS VARIABLE EXPENSES

Typically, your expenses can be divided into two main categories: fixed and variable expenses. You might not realize this now, but having knowledge of how to classify your expenses will actually allow you to budget your money better. You will know how to develop more effective spending strategies that allow you to manage your finances more effectively by understanding the inherent natures of your expenses. That's why it's imperative that you take some time to understand the differences between the two kinds of expenses and what money-saving tactics you can employ for each of them.

Fixed Expenses

Think of your fixed expenses as the money that you routinely spend every month which roughly rounds up to the same amount consistently. So, this would include internet plans, subscriptions, mortgages, car payments, rent payments, and insurance premiums. Of course, theoretically, it's possible for some of these expenses to fluctuate every once in a while, but they tend to stay consistent for the most part. This is why fixed expenses are always a lot easier to manage and budget for. You expect them to come every month and you know how much money you have to set aside in order for you to pay for them.

But how do you save money when it comes to your fixed expenses? Well, the first thing that you have to remind yourself is that just because they're fixed expenses doesn't mean that you always have to pay them. What that means is that you always have the capacity to cut off certain expenses in life in order to ease the burden of your finances. For example, if you find yourself in a precarious position with your finances, you are always free to cut certain fixed expenses like subscription services in order to save more money consistently. We've already talked about how much these *minor* expenses can add up to and cutting out even one or two of them can make a significant difference.

Usually, your fixed expenses are what make up most of your spending budget every month. That's why you should try to focus most of your energy toward lessening these expenses to the best of your abilities. It isn't even going to require much sacrifice on your part to try to lower your fixed expenses. For example, you could always try sniffing around for better insurance plans that have cheaper premiums. You can also browse for cell phone or internet plans that offer better deals and will allow you to have more savings. Try to scrimp as much money as you can with your fixed expenses and it's really going to add up over time to a significant chunk of change.

Variable Expenses

To put it simply, variable expenses are any kind of expenditures that you choose to make on a whim. For example, you buy a pair of shoes that you saw while you passed a store along the street one day. You go for a night out drinking with the buddies to celebrate a milestone of a friend. You decide to take the entire family out for a movie with snacks for everyone. On the way to work, you're feeling sleepy and so you decide to hop into a Starbucks to order your cup of coffee. These are all examples of variable expenses that you don't necessarily plan for, but can account for a big part of your budget just the same.

These kinds of expenses are considered *variable* because you don't typically know how much you would be spending on them on a month-to-month basis. For the most part, you can't anticipate how much money you would spend on drinks or dinners out with friends every month. It's all *variable*. Another classic example would be groceries. Most families out there don't have a consistent grocery budget for every month. Sometimes, it can be as little as $200 and on other months it can reach as high as $300. In this case, groceries become variable expenses even though you do them consistently.

Interestingly enough, variable costs are the types of expenses that people typically try to cut down on whenever they feel like they need to be saving more money. But the problem with making a conscious effort to cut down on variable expenses is that it's not always going to make the most dramatic impact on your financial health. This is because variable expenses, by nature, are inherently erratic. If you're just consciously trying to save in variable expenses every month, then it's all really going to depend on the situations that you're in as opposed to working on your fixed expenses that are always known and measurable.

However, that isn't to say that you shouldn't make an effort to minimize your variable expenses. You should still try to do so if you're looking to rehabilitate your finances. One good way to do this is to try to transform most of your variable expenses into fixed ones. If you notice a trend in your spending, then try to predict how that trend will be moving forward and budget for it appropriately. For example, try turning your grocery expenses into fixed expenses by allotting a specific budget for it every month. Set a cap for yourself with a slight buffer to allow for miscellaneous purchases. Try to never exceed that cap so that you stay consistent with how much you're spending. If you end up not using the entire amount, then you can always put it toward your savings and investments. And you don't have to do this with just your groceries. You can also set a cap on your shopping, dinners out, movies, and other variable expenses that you routinely do. This way, you're adding more order and structure to the way you spend your money.

PERSONAL STORY

For the last personal story of this book, I want to talk about another friend of mine who approached me to talk about her problems with money. She always told me that she was poor and that she was struggling to save. And so, I wanted to get to the root of her financial woes to try to figure out what she was doing wrong. As we were talking, I discovered a pattern of her just constantly engaging in a lot of unnecessary spending. For example, she had a tendency of being a procrastinator and she was always late whenever it came to filing taxes. Even though taxes were due on the 31st of March, she would typically file them some time around October. It wasn't just one year that she did this. This was something that she did consistently year after year. She ended up having to pay so many unnecessary penalties (which were quite hefty) even though she didn't have to.

If she had been paying more attention to her spending, then it probably would have been a different story. The thing is that she just didn't care about the penalties that were piling up and eating away at her money. She saw the taxes as necessary expenses anyway, she didn't pay much attention to the penalties. The exact figures were a blur to her even though they were rather significant. She was literally paying a few extra hundred dollars a year that she could have saved if she just cared enough to take a look at how much money she was wasting on these unnecessary penalties. This is why I always preach just how crucial it is to pay more attention to the way that you spend your money.

AFTERWORD

We've reached the end of the book and it's okay if you're feeling a little overwhelmed by all of the information that you've consumed so far. Personal finance is a very heavy topic, and well, as the name implies, it's a very personal journey. You're going to have to confront a lot of thoughts, beliefs, and habits that you have and they aren't always going to be comfortable. Exploring your personal finance philosophy is never easy because you will have to come to terms with the fact that you're not always doing the right thing and you have to rid yourself of old habits. But that's okay. That's an essential aspect of a person's growth and development. You always need to look at the parts of yourself that require improvement and show a willingness to grow from these lessons.

In this book, we talked about how important it is for you to practice good habits when it comes to the formation of your character and your overall makeup as an individual. While this book may have been focused on personal finance, you should know that the practicing of good habits is a principle that can carry over into other aspects of life. Habits can help you develop a routine that will eventually mold you into the person that you dream of becoming. Being grounded in a solid routine made up of good habits can help you achieve your goals, whether it be in finance, relationships, or your career.

Before closing this book, it might be best to do a quick runthrough of the major ideas that we covered here so far just to serve as a refresher. First, we talked about the major obstacles that people usually face when trying to achieve financial independence. Here, we talked about factors like debt, poor financial literacy and planning, and stress. These are all dangerous habits that you need to make sure that you don't practice because they are going to keep you from reaching your goals. Then, we talked about the simple steps that you could take to help you develop better habits with regard to your finances. We talked about some of the basic fundamental principles of financial responsibility and management. All of this served as foundational knowledge for the true meat of this book: the five approaches that lead to financial independence.

The first approach is for you to maintain your day job. It's a source of reliable income with a lot of added benefits. Yes, you don't want to slave away at your desk for a corporate behemoth for the rest of your life. But that doesn't mean that you need to quit so hastily. Take your time and gradually transition yourself into a life of financial independence. The second approach is for you to go on a spending diet. A lot of people seem to think that the key to getting rich is merely finding a way to earn more money. For some people, this is feasible and easy. It's also true. The more money you have coming in, then the likelier you will be to get rich. However, there's another side to the equation. You can also try to decrease your spending. Think of your expenditures as food. If you overindulge, you're going to end up getting fat and you risk developing obesity-related health conditions like heart disease, diabetes, hypertension, and even cancer. The only way for you to avoid these problems is to cut down on the food that you're eating. That's also what you need to do with your finances. You must cut down on your spending to maintain good financial health. The third approach is to save your money. You should never be content with just taking a casual or lackadaisical approach to saving your money. It has to be more intentional and methodical. We highlighted a few different saving plans that you can try out for yourself. But again, personal finance is a personal journey. This means that it's okay for you to tweak the plan to cater to your specific conditions, needs, and goals. In the fourth approach, we talked about the movement of your money or cash flow. We discussed that it's not enough for you to merely know that you're earning money. It's important that you know how much money you're getting and where it's all coming from. Additionally, you must also acquaint yourself with how you use your money. How much money are you spending and where is it all going? It's this kind of attention to detail that is crucial to you developing your financial literacy and helping you achieve your personal financial goals. And the final approach to achieving financial independence has to do with you making a more conscious effort to avoid unnecessary spending. You must learn the differences between fixed and variable expenses. Wherever you can, try to trim the fat within your spending. Even making these seemingly small changes can have very deep and profound changes over time.

Change is definitely not an easy process, especially if you happen to be someone who is so set in your ways. You can be living an extremely toxic lifestyle and be okay with it because you're too afraid to make the changes that are necessary to better yourself. Understand that there are many who understand your initial reluctance to change your ways and adopt a new way of living. But just because it's difficult doesn't mean that you shouldn't do it. When it comes to self-improvement, the pros are always going to outweigh the cons. You just need to find that courage and resolve within yourself to actually commit to your goals and transform yourself into the person you want to become.

Hopefully, this book will have equipped you with all of the foundational information that you need to get the ball rolling and create a better life for yourself. Again, it was a lot of information, and it's okay if you go back to this book every once in a while just to refresh yourself on everything that you've learned. What's important for now is that you start. Ignite that spark for change within you and watch as you slowly morph your life into the one that you've always been dreaming of. And when you get that first taste of success, you'll get hooked. There's a certain energy that comes with being able to achieve something in life and that energy will keep you going. You'll become addicted to that feeling of fulfillment and self-actualization. It's this addiction that will keep you committed to your routine. It's what will keep you going forward. Before you even realize it, you'll find yourself smashing your goals and making news ones as you continue to press forward. You will have created a new life for yourself that's grounded in the philosophy of self-improvement. And it all started with you developing good habits.

A SPECIAL GIFT FOR MY READERS

Included with your purchase of this book is our Bonus Content,

7 Ways to Challenge Your Self-Control.

This booklet is a training for you to try with small day-to-day habits before you move on to making big changes in your life.

These mini challenges can help you improve your health, live minimalistically and can help you save more money!

Click the link below and let us know which email address to deliver to

https://benjamintaylor.activehosted.com/f/1

ABOUT THE AUTHOR

Before you can get to the meat of the book, you might want to learn more about where all this information is coming from. In the age of digital information, it's so easy to just fall into the trap of false gurus and self-proclaimed experts on the internet who claim that they have all the knowledge you need for you to be successful. But a lot of the time, these people are just clamoring for exposure even though there isn't really any weight to their claims or to their experiences. That certainly isn't the case for Benjamin Taylor.

Benjamin used to work a regular nine-to-five day job just like most other people in the labor force. He had first-hand experience of living paycheck to paycheck and he understood what it was like to be stuck in the cycle of a toxic rat race. He worked for a large corporation that thrived off the labor of its workers and it almost seemed to him that even though his company was growing, he was staying stagnant as an individual. Over time, he came to the realization that he wasn't happy with having to work eight hours a day only to go home at night feeling too tired and weary to do anything else. He hated how he had to ask his superiors at work for permission to take a break or go on a vacation that he knew he deserved. Benjamin went through all of the trials and tribulations that many common workers are currently experiencing.

Once he realized that, he decided to make a change in his life. Benjamin adopted a new approach to allocating his time and efforts. He readjusted his mindset and decided that it wasn't enough that he was living paycheck to paycheck. With some research and a commitment to reshuffling his habits, Benjamin abandoned his old life and got straight to work on building his new one. Nowadays, Benjamin is a full-time entrepreneur who has full control over his time and income. He is also now exploring his passion for writing and sharing his story to others who might be interested in a change in their lives as well.

Over the years, Benjamin has managed to accumulate a wealth of knowledge when it comes to business operations and personal finances. Through his experiences, Benjamin was forced to learn some very valuable lessons (sometimes, the hard way) about how to keep a business afloat and how to make it thrive. He studied business for more than eight years and has worked for various organizations with diverse operation frameworks and philosophical strategies. All of his experiences have helped equip him with the knowledge and wisdom that he needed to lift his own business off the ground. While working as an entrepreneur, Benjamin discovered the real value of financial literacy and how one's mindset is key to achieving success in that field. He experienced just how stressful it can be to have to deal with financial woes and he discovered a blueprint to help relieve himself of these stresses.

By writing this book, Benjamin has chosen to share this blueprint and influence as many people as possible to achieve the same kind of success that he has amassed for himself. In this book, Benjamin will talk candidly about his own experiences and the principles and lessons that he derived from them. He hopes that by sharing his knowledge, he can help people avoid the same mistakes that he had encountered in the path while also practicing the good habits that allowed him to eventually succeed. Benjamin self-admittedly understands that his renewed mindset managed to open countless doors of opportunity for him and he wants the same for all of his readers. This book is essentially Benjamin's love letters to people who dream of a life beyond just working from nine to five and living paycheck to paycheck. This book is for those who dream and those who are willing to do whatever it takes to succeed.

REFERENCES

Amadeo, K., & Estevez, E. (2021, March 26). *Consumer debt statistics, causes and impact*. The Balance; The Balance. https://www.thebalance.com/consumer-debt-statistics-causes-and-impact-3305704

Brooks, A. (2016, May 20). *A Payoff^{TM} study: Financial stress causes PTSD-Like symptoms in 1 in 4 Americans*. CardRates.com. https://www.cardrates.com/news/payoff-study-on-financial-stress/

Cressy, G. (2020, March 21). *The (super) power of habits and routines*. Grotto Network. https://grottonetwork.com/navigate-life/career-and-finance/why-habits-are-important/

Fox, M. (2020, April 16). *Coronavirus crisis is causing financial stress for nearly 9 in 10 Americans*. CNBC. https://www.cnbc.com/2020/04/16/coronavirus-crisis-causing-financial-stress-for-near-9-in-10-americans.html

Frankel, M., & Rosen, K. (2019, October 4). *Credit card debt statistics for 2020 | The Ascent*. The Motley Fool.

https://www.fool.com/the-ascent/research/credit-card-debt-statistics/

Friedman, Z. (2021, February 20). *Student loan debt statistics in 2021: A record $1.7 trillion*. Forbes. https://www.forbes.com/sites/zackfriedman/2021/02/20/student-loan-debt-statistics-in-2021-a-record-17-trillion/#:~:text=Student%20loan%20debt%20in%202021

Fu, C. (2021, February 15). *32 must-know financial literacy statistics in 2021*. Possible Finance. https://www.possiblefinance.com/blog/financial-literacy-statistics/

Jones, J. (2021, February 5). *Average car payment / loan statistics 2021* (D. Sheppard & A. Williams, Eds.). LendingTree. https://www.lendingtree.com/auto/debt-statistics/#:~:text=Auto%20debt%20makes%20up%205

Mission to Save. (2021, January 1). *Best way to save this year with a 365 day savings challenge*. Mission: To Save. https://missiontosave.com/best-way-to-save-this-year-with-a-365-day-savings-challenge/#:~:text=Here

Morah, C. (2020, March 22). *Evaluating your personal financial statement*. Investopedia. https://www.investopedia.com/articles/pf/08/evaluate-personal-financial-statement.asp

Pant, P. (2020a, May 4). *Understanding the difference between fixed and variable expenses* (S. Anderson, Ed.). The Balance. https://www.thebalance.com/what-s-the-difference-between-fixed-and-variable-expenses-453774

Pant, P. (2020b, June 7). *How much should I save each month?* (M. James, Ed.). The Balance. https://www.thebalance.com/how-much-money-should-you-save-each-month-453930

Pendola, R. (2020, September 7). *Are you financially self-aware?* Medium. https://themakingofamillionaire.com/are-you-financially-self-aware-3c2d34a83522

Resendiz, J. (2021, March 22). *Average credit card debt in America.* ValuePenguin. https://www.valuepenguin.com/average-credit-card-debt

Rosenberg, E. (2017, March 2). *5 reasons you should keep your day job.* Due. https://due.com/blog/5-reasons-keep-day-job/

ZUCCHI, K. (2019). *Why financial literacy is so important.* Investopedia. https://www.investopedia.com/articles/investing/100615/why-financial-literacy-and-education-so-important.asp

www.ingramcontent.com/pod-product-compliance
Lightning Source LLC
Chambersburg PA
CBHW020911080526
44589CB00011B/537